REVIEWS

> Nothing is safe from Michael Chanley's curious and imaginative gaze, including bees. Chanley's playful but godly inquiries into their habits remind us once more how God is at work literally everywhere. A wonderfully creative and deliciously sweet read!

- DR. NEAL WINDHAM
PROFESSOR EMERITUS, LINCOLN CHRISTIAN UNIVERSITY

> Over the years I have watched as a hobby farm turned into a source of Holy truths. Hope & Honey Bees is Michael's genuine expression of Biblical principles told through the interesting, intentional lives honey bees live.
>
> Michael does a masterful job of revealing the truth of verses such as Job 12:7-10 & Romans 1:20, as he unpacks the undeniable gospel lessons our Lord has locked away in the lives, rhythms, and relationships of the honey bee. It was interesting to learn so much about the art of Beekeeping; and, I was truly blessed to learn so much about the presence of God.
>
> Upon completing this book your hope in Christ will be strengthened & you will never look at a jar of honey the same way again.

- BRAD TATE
LEAD PASTOR AGAPÉ CITY CHURCH, HOWELL MI

REVIEWS

> The connection between the spiritual and natural is the playground for spiritual formation, and Michael does an excellent job connecting the two worlds thus promoting a formational experience for the reader.

- CALEB BROWN

AUTHOR OF "STARTING MINISTRY" AND "THEOLOGY FOR GEN-Z"

> People of all generations want to possess hope. In a wonderful and clear way, Michael shares his beekeeping analogy that explains not only God's design for honeybees but also for our lives. This is affirming for those who know Christ and for those who are "Pre-Christian." It's an easy to understand story. Your friends will thank you for sharing this book with them.

- GARY B. DIXON

30 YEARS WITH DAVID C. COOK PUBLISHING

FOUNDER & CEO EMERITUS OF NORTHWEST MINISTRY CONFERENCE

> Hope & Honeybees will be a source of enlightenment, encouragement, and empowerment to live your faith in a real and authentic manner. Michael engagingly shares his experiences and the lessons he's learned as a beekeeper. For me, the best part about reading through these lessons is knowing that my long-time friend actually practices what he teaches as a man of great faith, love and compassion. I would encourage everyone to read this gem of a book!

- GREG BAIRD

FOUNDER/PRESIDENT, LEAD BETTER TODAY, LLC

REVIEWS

> Michael's words on hope are inspiring; and, I believe that many parallels can be drawn from beekeeping for our everyday life. As I was reading, I was struck by the questions: is there a God, is there an afterlife, is it more than just hope?
>
> In beekeeping, you don't need to find or see the queen to know if you have a well sustaining colony of honey bees. You look for indicators; eggs, larvae and capped brood, that is all you need to answer the question: 'Is there a queen?'
>
> In our lives, although we can't see God; there is so much of His good works around us to prove He exists. Even with all the bad around us, faith and hope are tools to help us when we encounter a time of 'doubt and hardship.'

- JOHN SCHELLENBERGER
PRESIDENT OF THE BEEKEEPERS OF INDIANA
FLOYD COUNTY, INDIANA COMMISSIONER

> I've known Michael for years, and in *Hope and Honeybees: Lessons of Faith from a Local Beekeeper*, he brilliantly uncovers profound wisdom in the world of honeybees. These tiny creatures teach us about unwavering hope and resilience. Michael, a local beekeeper and pastor, seamlessly blends spiritual insights with the bee's life, offering a unique and enlightening perspective. This book beautifully connects the bee's world to our own, reminding us of the importance of faith, unity, and purpose. *Hope and Honeybees* is a captivating blend of science, spirituality, and storytelling that will leave you inspired and connected to the natural world. A must-read for anyone seeking a deeper understanding of life's lessons.

- JUSTYN SMITH
STORY CATALYST, PLAINJOE STUDIOS
AUTHOR OF "KIDMIN, TRUST & PIXIE DUST"

ALSO BY MICHAEL J. CHANLEY

Escape - The Traps of Christianity

Escape - The Traps of Christianity Journal

Chasing WHALES - A Spiritual Dive With Jonah

Collaborate: Family + Church

The Art of Parenting - Nurturing Happy, Confident, and Resilient Children

Hope & Honeybees

Hope & Honeybees

Lessons of Faith From a Local Beekeeper

Michael J. Chanley

Wyatt Chanley

Churchlit Publishing

Hope & Honeybees - Lessons of Faith From a Local Beekeeper
Copyright © 2023 by Michael J. Chanley

All rights reserved. No part of this book may be reproduced in any manner whatsoever without written permission except in the case of brief quotations embodied in critical articles and reviews. This book or parts thereof may not be reproduced in any form, stored in any retrieval system, or transmitted in any form by any means—electronic, mechanical, photocopy, recording, or otherwise—without prior written permission of the publisher, except as provided by United States of America copyright law. While the author has made every effort to provide accurate Internet addresses and references to sources at the time of publication, neither the publisher nor the author assumes any responsibility for errors or for changes that occur after publication.

First Printing, 2023

Published in the United States by Churchlit Publishing.

Author: Michael J. Chanley
Editor: Wyatt Chanley
Cover Design: Michael J. Chanley & Cori Horvath
Author Photo: Kevin Mosier & Eden Chanley

All Scripture quotations, unless otherwise indicated, are taken from the Holy Bible, New International Version®, NIV®. Copyright ©1973, 1978, 1984, 2011 by Biblica, Inc.™ Used by permission of Zondervan. All rights reserved worldwide. www.zondervan.com The "NIV" and "New International Version" are trademarks registered in the United States Patent and Trademark Office by Biblica, Inc.™
In some cases, the author has made modifications for clarification. This will appear as text that has been bolded or bracketed. Some additional line breaks were added for formatting continuity.

Hardcover ISBN: 979-8-9892277-2-3
Paperback ISBN: 979-8-9892277-4-7
Ebook ISBN: 979-8-9892277-5-4

Subjects: Christianity, devotional, hope, honeybees, culture, faith, love, Jesus Christ, Christian living, spirituality

Bulk sales discounts may be available. To inquire, please contact sales@churchlit.com.
For speaking engagements, email: emersen@churchlit.com.

CONTENTS

DEDICATION xiii

1 Hope 1

2 Keeper 11

3 Creator 17

4 Enemy 22

5 Despair 27

6 Stages 32

7 Beatitudes 37

8 Swarm 58

9 Legacy 63

10 Superorganism 83

11 Unity 91

12 Honey 104

CONTENTS

13 | Harvest 110

14 | Love 121

FOOTNOTES 139
ABOUT THE AUTHOR 156

*Special thanks to Spring Valley Beekeepers Club and
the Beekeepers of Indiana.*

I've learned so much from our community.

My bees and I truly appreciate you!

*For Tunnel Hill Christian Church and
the hope you share with our community.*

For Rose, Wyatt, Brooke, Emersen, Eden, and our family.

For all who pick up this book to give it a read.

*I sincerely thank each of you for being a source of
encouragement and inspiration.
You have all my love!*

1

Hope

What is hope?

Attempting to define hope leads to more profound questions.

What do you place your hope in?

What do you hope for?

Does your hope withstand the challenges of a world filled with despair?

The Biblical sense of hope differs significantly from the secularized idea of hope. For example, the earthly concept of hope becomes evident in how we often reply to expectations with the phrase "I hope so…"

It's not rooted in anything other than our indirect optimism.

Will my car start today?

I hope so.

Will there be enough money for me to retire?

I hope so.

Will it snow for Christmas?

I hope so.

"I hope so…" expresses a general sense of optimistic expectation of the future.

Biblical hope expresses this same optimism, but faith-filled hope is grounded in our relationship with Christ. Our hope is confirmed and affirmed by faith, and we have real hope through a relationship with a God who is always faithful.

God is always faithful.

He says He will do something, and He always does it. Our hope is grounded in His character.

John Piper, a well-known Christian pastor, speaker, and author, succinctly defines the Biblical definition of hope. He says hope:

> "… DOES NOT IMPLY UNCERTAINTY OR LACK OF ASSURANCE. INSTEAD, BIBLICAL HOPE IS A CONFIDENT EXPECTATION AND DESIRE FOR SOMETHING GOOD IN THE FUTURE. THERE IS MORAL CERTAINTY IN IT."[1]

Simply put, Biblical Hope is confidence in God's continued faithfulness.

Our hope in Christ is not in vain. It is of great value. Because God has always kept His word, we are well assured of an eternal future when we place our hope and faith in Jesus Christ.

It's far better than the hope we put in our car's extended warranty.

Hope in Anything?

An interviewer once asked Elvis Presley about a famous necklace he wore around his neck. The King of Rock and Roll was "a devout follower of God." "He wore a cross around his neck, yes... he also wore a necklace bearing the Star of David, and another with the Hebrew word "chai" – which translates to "life" in English."[2] When asked why he wore a mixture of religious symbols, he would say, "I don't want to get left out of heaven on a technicality..."[3]

Elvis wanted assurance of his future hope in God.

However, he was hedging his bets. He wanted to cover all of the bases.

Elvis's pluralistic approach to hope makes for a great story but is a terribly problematic way to live our lives.

Placing our bet in everything available begs a challenging question: Do you honestly believe Jesus is the hope God has given us or not?

Are you hoping in any random thing, or are you hopefully turning to the One thing?

Our hope in God's provision is not a gamble. We don't have to question our faith and always be concerned whether or not we have picked the correct numbers, the proper sequence of rituals, the right denomination, the best church, or the popular gods.

We have absolute assurance in God's Word through God Himself. It is the power of knowing Jesus Christ.

Therefore, when we ask the hard questions of our faith, questions that lead us to a sense of hopefulness for eternity:

Is there an afterlife?

Will I go to heaven?

Will I be forgiven?

Does God love me?

Our response to such uncertain questions need not be, "Well, I sure hope so."

No.

Our hope in God's provision is certainty. It comes from knowing His Word is truth, and He is trustworthy.

He is the God who provides.

His provision and goodness underscore our unwavering hope.

The Gift of Hope

Matthew's gospel shows the fulfillment of generations of hope from the start. The genealogical introduction of chapter one illustrates the long line of families that had all previously waited for the promised Messiah.

Matthew chapter one helps us to see that Jesus is the fulfillment of past hopes.

He is the One prophesied as King and Redeemer.

He is the fulfillment of God's promises.

Jesus is the gift of hope made flesh.

Matthew, the first Book of the New Testament, is written to explain the good news of Jesus to the Jews. In this sense, it is a gospel for the people of God. It is for those familiar with the history and traditions of the Jewish faith and for people who have some understanding of the Old Testament. For this reason, the writer of Matthew takes special care to explain how Jesus fulfilled the prior Law and the promises made to the people of Israel by God.

When we read Matthew's text with this understanding, it has special meaning and significance. Even the quite boring genealogy at the beginning comes to life with renewed purpose.

For context, the people of Israel had all but given up hope of their Messiah coming.

They despaired under the political power and subjugation of Roman rule. The Romans worshiped a pantheon of gods, and it must have seemed an insult to the Jewish belief in the One True God. Worse, the Romans ruled over Israel and all their subjugated lands harshly and cruelly.

Yet, amid great suffering, God breathed life.

Into despair, Christ was born.

Into despair, the promised Messiah arrived.

Into despair, God stepped onto Earth as the man, Jesus of Nazareth.

Yes.

In a despairing world, hope illuminated the darkness.

Matthew writes to the heart of a nation stumbling in the night, to hurting and broken people.

Matthew writes to explain their fulfilled hope.

Matthew writes to share the good news of Jesus.

Light came into the world, and that light became hope for all!

Take a moment to let this prophecy foretelling Jesus wash over you. Imagine hearing these words read aloud by generations waiting for God to deliver on His promise.

Isaiah 42 foreshadows the hopeful coming of the Messiah.

> [1] "HERE IS MY SERVANT, WHOM I UPHOLD,
> MY CHOSEN ONE IN WHOM I DELIGHT;
> I WILL PUT MY SPIRIT ON HIM,
> AND HE WILL BRING JUSTICE TO THE NATIONS.
> ...
> [4] HE WILL NOT FALTER OR BE DISCOURAGED
> TILL HE ESTABLISHES JUSTICE ON EARTH.
> IN HIS TEACHING THE ISLANDS WILL PUT THEIR HOPE."
> [5] THIS IS WHAT GOD THE LORD SAYS—
> THE CREATOR OF THE HEAVENS, WHO STRETCHES THEM OUT,
> WHO SPREADS OUT THE EARTH WITH ALL THAT SPRINGS FROM IT,
> WHO GIVES BREATH TO ITS PEOPLE,
> AND LIFE TO THOSE WHO WALK ON IT:
> [6] "I, THE LORD, HAVE CALLED YOU IN RIGHTEOUSNESS;
> I WILL TAKE HOLD OF YOUR HAND.
> I WILL KEEP YOU AND WILL MAKE YOU
> TO BE A COVENANT FOR THE PEOPLE
> AND A LIGHT FOR THE GENTILES,
> [7] TO OPEN EYES THAT ARE BLIND,
> TO FREE CAPTIVES FROM PRISON
> AND TO RELEASE FROM THE DUNGEON
> THOSE WHO SIT IN DARKNESS.[4]

Isaiah's prophecy provides hope for a promised Messiah to come and deliver the people of God. It is a powerful foretelling of Jesus' ministry. The Prophet Isaiah "ministered to God's people roughly from 742 to 700 b.c. in an era of great political tumult."[5] In an era of chaos and despair, God's messenger proclaimed a word of hope.

Keep in mind, that these prophetic words were written some 700 years before Jesus was even born.

Read verse 1 of Isaiah 42 once more,

> [1] I WILL PUT MY SPIRIT ON HIM,
> AND HE WILL BRING JUSTICE TO THE NATIONS.[6]

Matthew understood the words of Isaiah. He references this prophecy of Isaiah in chapter 12, verse 21.

> [21] IN HIS NAME THE NATIONS WILL PUT THEIR HOPE.[7]

The prophecy is not "Well, I kinda hope so…"

No.

It is not, "Maybe that will happen…"

It is a confident and sure hope.

It is the fulfillment of promises made by a God who backs up His Words with action.

Beginning with the genealogical record of hopeful believers, Matthew's Gospel becomes a testament to God's faithful fulfillment of His promises. Matthew is showing us Jesus is the promised One. This intentionality reveals the faithfulness of God.

It is, again, His faithfulness that we put our hope in. He says He will do something, and He does it.

Through His very nature, we find real hope.

Matthew gives us an explanation of Christ's birth as the fulfillment of generations of hope. The ages accounted for in Matthew's opening chapter help demonstrate God's past fulfillment of promises. This hope-fulfilled also gives the Christmas story, the next bit of text in Matthew's introduction, much more significance.

With hope-filled lenses, we can understand Joseph and Mary so much better.

Matthew 1:18 begins the story of Joseph, the adopted father of Jesus.

> [18] THIS IS HOW THE BIRTH OF JESUS THE MESSIAH CAME ABOUT: HIS MOTHER MARY WAS PLEDGED TO BE MARRIED TO JOSEPH, BUT BEFORE THEY CAME TOGETHER, SHE WAS FOUND TO BE PREGNANT THROUGH THE HOLY SPIRIT.
> [19] BECAUSE JOSEPH HER HUSBAND WAS FAITHFUL TO THE LAW, AND YET DID NOT WANT TO EXPOSE HER TO PUBLIC DISGRACE, HE HAD IN MIND TO DIVORCE HER QUIETLY.
> [20] BUT AFTER HE HAD CONSIDERED THIS, AN ANGEL OF THE LORD APPEARED TO HIM IN A DREAM AND SAID, "JOSEPH SON OF DAVID, DO NOT BE AFRAID TO TAKE MARY HOME AS YOUR WIFE, BECAUSE WHAT IS CONCEIVED IN HER IS FROM THE HOLY SPIRIT.
> [21] SHE WILL GIVE BIRTH TO A SON, AND YOU ARE TO GIVE HIM THE NAME JESUS, BECAUSE HE WILL SAVE HIS PEOPLE FROM THEIR SINS."

²² ALL THIS TOOK PLACE TO FULFILL WHAT THE LORD HAD SAID THROUGH THE PROPHET: ²³ "THE VIRGIN WILL CONCEIVE AND GIVE BIRTH TO A SON, AND THEY WILL CALL HIM IMMANUEL" (WHICH MEANS "GOD WITH US").
²⁴ WHEN JOSEPH WOKE UP, HE DID WHAT THE ANGEL OF THE LORD HAD COMMANDED HIM AND TOOK MARY HOME AS HIS WIFE. ²⁵ BUT HE DID NOT CONSUMMATE THEIR MARRIAGE UNTIL SHE GAVE BIRTH TO A SON. AND HE GAVE HIM THE NAME JESUS.[8]

Immanuel.

God with us.

Jesus.

In His name, the nations will put their hope.

Again, Biblical hope is not hope casually tossed at the lowest common denominator. Nor is it hope in a possible good outcome. Certainly, it is not "I hope so… rolling-of-the-dice-type of hope."

It is hope that is grounded in generations of faithfulness.

It is hope proven by the fulfillment of prophecies.

It is hope connected to faith and the demonstrated love of God; **a gift of hope, fulfilled in the name of Jesus!**

Therefore, I believe it was this hope, revealed to Joseph, the Earthly father of Jesus, that moved him to act with compassion towards Mary. Joseph's faith moved to action as Mary, his betrothed wife, delivered God's plan for redemption. Mary delivered hope in something Joseph couldn't fathom, but he accepted it on the Word of God's messengers.

Then, Jesus grew up and became hope for all!

And so, as we begin to think about the idea of hope together, what do you put your hope in?

As followers of Christ, we need not say, "I hope so…" regarding our eternal destination. We have the distinct blessing of true hope, with the assured confidence of the One who is always faithful, perfectly just, and unendingly filled with love and mercy.

May we hope in Him completely!

2

Keeper

Beekeeping is born of hope.

One could say it is a reckless type of hope filled with optimism. If so, beekeeping is a great comparison of placing our hope in something worldly and out of control.

As hobbies go, keeping bees requires a good bit of optimism and no shortage of effort.

Like all agricultural endeavors, there are no guarantees. One may never even harvest a single ounce of honey. Most first-year beekeepers will lose all of their original colonies. Experienced keepers will tell you it is a success if three-quarters of the hives survive winter.

I once heard a beekeeper say that to keep bees is a hopeful endeavor, but it's hardly a get-rich-quick scheme. One can make money keeping bees; some large bee farms do pretty well. Generally speaking, however, the easiest way to become a millionaire with honeybees is to start as a billionaire.

Beekeeping is a costly endeavor. Just like all skills, it requires time to learn. There is also the upfront cost of purchasing hive boxes, frames, extractors, and all of the necessary specialized equipment needed to manage bees. Then, you must invest more time on a seemingly never-ending list of to-dos. It is costly work to build a successful apiary.

Despite all of this effort, the bees will do what the bees will do.

For anyone working with honeybees: Hoping in a harvest is filled with uncertainty.

This chance taking makes hope feel like a faith-based gamble in an unknown tomorrow.

Hope, therefore, becomes expensive.

Yet, hope also presents an opportunity.

Rosecroft Farmstead

Nestled in the gently rolling hills of southern Indiana, just north of Louisville, Kentucky, is my family's hobby farm. Rosecroft Farmstead sits on 16 acres, flanked by a small forest, a hidden driveway, and a seemingly constant gentle breeze that rolls down the valley and toward the Ohio River.

In the 1850s, this region emerged as a newly settled part of the American landscape. The old farmhouse that my family and I began to restore in the fall of 2020 has sat here for at least 150 years. Its hand-cut stone cellar and hand-hewn beams also tell a story of hope. Over the years, the house was shaped by each owner's dreams. From what we can tell, it has been remodeled and added onto at least six different times. From a tiny farmhouse, bedrooms got extended, bathrooms were added, a second floor was raised, and eventually, a sunroom was attached to the North side of the house. As we undertook our remodeling project, we were blessed to uncover bits and pieces of that story.

If it sounds quaint and idyllic, it is. We hope it will be a place for us to finish our days together as a family.

Our move to this old farmhouse was also born of hope.

We moved here dreaming of a more peaceful way of life, free of the busyness of the suburbs, and hoping for a place closer to nature. We desired to be closer to God or to have, as my seminary professor calls it, "A more pastoral existence of simplicity."

In the months before we moved, during those dark days of quarantine and isolation caused by the COVID-19 pandemic, my oldest daughter had turned me on to honeybees. Watching videos on YouTube became a new favorite late-night pastime. It became a bit of a fascination that eventually led to reading books and joining a local beekeepers club.

By the time we sold our home in Louisville and bought our farm, I had spent over a thousand hours researching all I could about beekeeping. I was hooked.

With a donation of equipment from an elder at church, a small investment in some used equipment, and a great deal of hope in harvesting some sweet, sweet honey, I set up a bee yard, or apiary, at our farm.

Setting up a place to keep bees requires some creative thinking. Consideration has to be made for the safest place to locate the colony and a lot of prep work goes into creating a healthy habitat.

Amongst the first decisions a beekeeper makes is location. Where will you place the hives for the honeybees? A good apiary faces the morning sun. This allows the bees to soak up the benefit of the early morning rays as they start their day off kissed with a warm breeze.

There is also equipment that has to be purchased before the bees arrive. Most beekeepers use a style of equipment pioneered "in 1851 by Reverend Lorenzo Lorraine Langstroth."[9] His innovative approach to beekeeping is now the default option for commercial and hobbyist keepers.

A typical Langstroth hive kit consists of a bottom board, a deep hive box complete with frames, an inside cover, an outside cover, and an entrance reducer.[10] A stand capable of holding the weight of the bees and equipment also has to be purchased or built and put in place. Finally, the ground under the stand needs to be leveled and prepped.

Supers, or boxes that go above the hive box, also have to be purchased. These medium or small-sized boxes require frames as well. To prevent the queen bee from laying eggs in the honey-producing areas, a queen excluder also has to be purchased.

Additionally, there are feeders for supplementing the bees' food supply during the late-summer dearth or dry season. These specialized feeders should be bought in advance. A good beekeeper will always have some pollen and sugar on hand to help the bees in a challenging season.

There is the personal equipment the beekeeper must buy for their safety. Honeybees will protect their colony, and their sting, although not terrible, is better avoided. At a minimum, keepers need a veil and gloves. A full beekeeping suit is much safer. You'll also need to buy a smoker and a hive tool for doing inspections. A journal will come in handy to keep track of what is happening in your colonies. As an added precaution, we keep an epi-pen on hand at our farm. You never know when your body could react adversely to one bee sting, never mind if a visitor should get stung or if someone was unfortunate enough to be attacked multiple times.

Finally, and this would be hard to overlook, you must purchase a bee colony. Yes, you can catch them in the wild, but most first-year keepers invest in a package of honeybees to help ensure they get off to a great start.

As I said, beekeeping is expensive.

Altogether, you'll need to invest almost $1,000 just to get started. That's a grand out-of-pocket with the commitment of long work hours in the hot sun, the constant threat of getting stung, and no guarantee of ever harvesting an ounce of honey.

Sounds fun, right?

Trust me, I'm not trying to sell you on starting a bee farm. Instead, I want you to see the great deal of hope required to get started.

Beekeeping is born of an uncertain hope.

In this sense, hope is a feeling of expectation or trust in a positive outcome. It is looking forward to an imagined future with optimism. We often think of hope as girded in our understanding of faith and a deep belief in something more than what we can see directly in front of us.

One could say it takes a spark of creative hope to even become a beekeeper. As a keeper, the start of a journey means creating an environment for the bees to thrive. A keeper puts faith in their efforts and the honeybees. Once the prep work is done, the equipment is in place, the bees are ordered, and the plans are in motion, there's not much else to do but pray the bees do their job.

Beekeeping is uncertain hope.

MICHAEL J. CHANLEY

By contrasting the efforts required to become a keeper of bees with our world's intentional, hopeful design, we can better understand certain hope.

3

Creator

Our universe was born of hope.

Physically speaking, our universe began in nothingness. There was void except for the loving intentions of a hope-filled Creator.

> IN THE BEGINNING, GOD CREATED THE HEAVENS AND THE EARTH. 2 THE EARTH WAS WITHOUT FORM AND VOID, AND DARKNESS WAS OVER THE FACE OF THE DEEP. AND THE SPIRIT OF GOD WAS HOVERING OVER THE FACE OF THE WATERS. 3 AND GOD SAID, "LET THERE BE LIGHT," AND THERE WAS LIGHT.[11]

Into complete darkness and the void of formlessness, God spoke. From nothing came light.

The Genesis story then begins with the perfection of Eden. All of life and humanity is spoken into existence by God.

From nothing, everything was created.

Whether you read the Genesis account as metaphorical or believe it is a literal, day-by-day accounting of God's creative process, one thing is certain: It tells His story. Genesis puts God at the center. God is in control, and his glory is on full display.

We, the created, are then born into His hope-filled reality.

God, like the beekeeper establishing a home for a colony of honeybees, put the sun, moon, and stars into place. He ordered all things.

The consistencies discovered through scientific study reveal the physical properties of a habitat designed for us. For example, we can know the sun will rise each morning because the laws of perpetual motion, created by the designer, mean our world will continue to turn, and the sun will continue to burn. We can trust the laws of gravity, time, and thermodynamics to persist, even as our understanding of them becomes more complete.

To this sentiment, the writer of Psalm 19 declares God's creation in the most beautiful terms.

We read:

> GOD'S GLORY IS ON TOUR IN THE SKIES,
> GOD-CRAFT ON EXHIBIT ACROSS THE HORIZON.
> MADAME DAY HOLDS CLASSES EVERY MORNING,
> PROFESSOR NIGHT LECTURES EACH EVENING.
> THEIR WORDS AREN'T HEARD,
> THEIR VOICES AREN'T RECORDED,
> BUT THEIR SILENCE FILLS THE EARTH:
> UNSPOKEN TRUTH IS SPOKEN EVERYWHERE.

That "unspoken truth" is the very nature of creation. It all declares the goodness of a God with hope in His design.

The Psalmist continues with an analogy showing how we are wed to His hopeful creations.

> GOD MAKES A HUGE DOME
> FOR THE SUN—A SUPERDOME!
> THE MORNING SUN'S A NEW HUSBAND
> LEAPING FROM HIS HONEYMOON BED,
> THE DAYBREAKING SUN AN ATHLETE
> RACING TO THE TAPE.
> THAT'S HOW GOD'S WORD VAULTS ACROSS THE SKIES
> FROM SUNRISE TO SUNSET,
> MELTING ICE, SCORCHING DESERTS,
> WARMING HEARTS TO FAITH.

We discover the result of our creation in realizing God's complete goodness. All we see points to Him and supports our faith with the knowledge of a "lifetime guarantee."

> THE REVELATION OF GOD IS WHOLE
> AND PULLS OUR LIVES TOGETHER.
> THE SIGNPOSTS OF GOD ARE CLEAR
> AND POINT OUT THE RIGHT ROAD.
> THE LIFE-MAPS OF GOD ARE RIGHT,
> SHOWING THE WAY TO JOY.
> THE DIRECTIONS OF GOD ARE PLAIN
> AND EASY ON THE EYES.
> GOD'S REPUTATION IS TWENTY-FOUR-CARAT GOLD,
> WITH A LIFETIME GUARANTEE.
> THE DECISIONS OF GOD ARE ACCURATE

DOWN TO THE NTH DEGREE.[12]

Woven into the creation of our world is a testament. There is a promise. Therefore, the universe becomes evidence of a faithful God for those open to believing. A loving Father who does what He says He will do.

He is, by definition, faithful.

Growing in our understanding of His nature, we realize God the Creator set things in place so that we, too, could experience the blessings of faith, the assurance of a hope-filled tomorrow.

Even the concepts of faith and hope become more evident as we understand God's nature. In Hebrews 11, the writer proclaims the closest definition of faith given to us in the Bible.

> NOW FAITH IS THE ASSURANCE OF THINGS HOPED FOR, THE CONVICTION OF THINGS NOT SEEN. 2 FOR BY IT THE PEOPLE OF OLD RECEIVED THEIR COMMENDATION. 3 BY FAITH WE UNDERSTAND THAT THE UNIVERSE WAS CREATED BY THE WORD OF GOD, SO THAT WHAT IS SEEN WAS NOT MADE OUT OF THINGS THAT ARE VISIBLE.[13]

In a powerful explanation of the nature of Jesus Christ, the Book of John echoes the sentiments of a loving creator, God, who created all things. John 1 begins this way:

> IN THE BEGINNING WAS THE WORD, AND THE WORD WAS WITH GOD, AND THE WORD WAS GOD. 2 HE WAS IN THE BEGINNING WITH GOD. 3 ALL THINGS WERE MADE THROUGH HIM, AND WITHOUT HIM WAS NOT ANYTHING MADE THAT WAS MADE. 4 IN HIM WAS LIFE, AND THE LIFE WAS THE LIGHT OF MEN.

Then, John continues with the Genesis-like language of hopeful light piercing the darkness in a manner that can not be overcome. Verse five continues,

> 5 THE LIGHT SHINES IN THE DARKNESS,
> AND THE DARKNESS HAS NOT OVERCOME IT.[14]

In the most personal way possible, God spoke into existence our world. Similar to the intentional steps of the beekeeper, planning their upcoming season, Creation screams a testimony of the intentionality of our God. The universe stretches our imagination and tests our faith to know He did it all for us.

We, like the universe, were born of hope.

However, hope has an enemy. Genesis and John both contrast the light of God's hopeful creation with the power it has over the darkness.

Therefore, it is worth asking, "What is the nature of this darkness we face?"

4

Enemy

If beekeeping is born of hope, perhaps so is despair.

Early in the summer, I found a heaping pile of dead bees at the entrance of my first hive. Their lifeless bodies piled up at the doorway and on the ground below. It was a mass about the size of a basketball cut in half.

Death had come for the bees.

As I looked closer, trying to understand the cause of their demise, I noticed several worker bees landing at the hive's entrance. They shook erratically and fell over. Some seemed to writhe in pain. The following day, there were more dead bees. The entire colony died within a week, and scavengers moved in to destroy what was left.

Everything pointed to a menacing, invisible culprit.

My bees died of poison.

Pesticides present a common challenge for beekeepers. Compared to other obstacles, these poisons are almost impossible to combat. Bees forage as far as three miles from their home. Their wide range means the dangers they face when foraging are impossible to control.

For example, our farm borders numerous subdivisions, private residences, and other farmlands. We can't influence what happens in the lawns, fields, and yards where our bees forage.

Whether it was a farmer who had sprayed their crops with an insecticide or a well-meaning neighbor treating their home for mosquitoes, the bees were the victims. Their lifeless bodies only remained a testament to one enemy's effects and the dangers facing our pollinators.

Poisons intended to eliminate harmful insects, like mosquitoes, also kill honeybees and many other beneficial insects. They are silent killers. As birds and other animals eat the dying insects, their toxic effects move up the food chain.

The survival of honeybees is not the only thing threatened.

Darwin's Theory of Evolution reveals a hard truth about the natural world: only the fit will survive. Thankfully, "fit" in this sense has less to do with how good you look when you show up at a pool party and is more concerned with one's ability to adapt in opposition to natural (or even unnatural) forces.

"Survival of the fittest" assumes adaptations in competition for limited resources or to protect one's existence. In the case of the honeybee, there is no shortage of threats to their existence. Their challenges range from limited resources, predation, and dangerous chemicals.

Basic animal husbandry encourages beekeepers to limit the negative effects of these negative forces. Doing so begins with understanding the challenges facing honeybees. There are many.

MICHAEL J. CHANLEY

War

According to the U. S. Department of Agriculture (USDA), several "major factors threatening honey bee health"... "can be divided into four general areas:

- parasites, predators, and pests
- pathogens
- poor nutrition
- Pesticides"

Together, these factors combine to create a toxic set of challenges that complicates honeybee health in the United States and elsewhere.[15]

Bees are constantly fighting for survival.

The Associated Press (AP) reported on research from the nonprofit research group Bee Informed Partnership. Writing in the summer of 2023 on the dramatic challenges facing honeybee colonies in the US, the AP said the 2022 loss of 48% of honeybee colonies was up from the "previous year's loss of 39% and the 12-year average of 39.6%."[16] However, the losses were "not as high as 2020-2021's 50.8% mortality rate."[17] Of the beekeepers surveyed, they reported to the "scientists that 21% loss over the winter is acceptable and more than three-fifths of beekeepers surveyed said their losses were higher than that."[18]

Parasites, predators, and pests include nearly microscopic creatures and much larger animals. On the tiny side of the scale are varroa mites. These hard-to-detect insects feed on the larval stage honeybees. Their presence weakens the hive and can eventually cause its collapse. Other insects can also attack bees. Hive beetles, wax moths, ants, yellow jackets, and spiders will prey on the honeybee. The larger predators, working as enemies of the bees, include mice, skunks, bears, and even feral children who might toss rocks just to "see what will happen." Yeah, you know who you are.

Pathogens are increasingly a challenge for honeybees. There is a growing threat of challenges from bacteria and fungi that attack bees. One such example, called American Foulbrood Disease, requires a beekeeper to destroy all of their infected equipment and bees, generally by fire.

Poor nutrition is a more natural challenge. It can stem from climatic changes, dry weather patterns, fire, or habitat destruction. Replacing native clovers and flowering plants with manicured landscapes can lead to bee starvation. Essentially, when no pollen-producing plants are in a given area, the honeybees starve.

Pesticides, as mentioned earlier, are especially sinister. These manufactured chemicals have brought devastation to pollinators and all of nature. Again, the source of this danger ranges from people who spray to kill mosquitoes in their yards to farmers treating their crops. The results for a colony of bees are almost always the same: painful death.

The bees are, of course, not without hope. Some studies suggest they are rebounding as government organizations have begun to restrict and prohibit certain types of pesticides.

Additionally, the honeybee is an incredibly well adapted creature. Their stinger is a weapon of defense used to defend their family. When they sting, they also release "an alarm pheromone that recruits nearby bees into mass stinging of the perceived threat."[19] They can attack with coordinated effort. A recent study suggests bees may even have a higher level of intelligence to allow them more adaptive protection against enemies. Collectively, they learn from their environment.

Stephen Buchmann "has studied bees for over 40 years." In a recent book: *What a Bee Knows: Exploring the Thoughts, Memories and Personalities of Bees*, he uncovers a deeper look into the "behaviour and psychology" of honeybees. Buchmann "argues that bees can demonstrate sophisticated emotions resembling optimism, frustration, playfulness and fear, traits more commonly associated with mammals." He goes on to report that some "experiments have shown bees can experience PTSD-like symptoms, recognize different human faces, process long-term memories while sleeping, and [they] maybe even dream."[20]

In short, Buchmann asserts that "Bees are self-aware, they're sentient, and they possibly have a primitive form of consciousness."[21] Despite their tiny brains and simpleness, he says bees "solve problems and can think."[22] Research suggests "Bees may even have a primitive form of subjective experiences."[23] Understanding bees as more complex helps us consider the stresses their environment puts on them. Like a family stretched too thin or facing a dire health diagnosis, the negative situation can cause trauma, eventually tearing them apart and destroying their ability to thrive.

For honeybees and beekeepers alike, knowing these enemies exist and are unrelenting in their attacks does not create hope.

The bees live in a constant state of attack. They exist in a state of war.

Their persistent enemies create the opposite of hope.

They unleash despair.

5

Despair

The opposite of hope is despair.

The dictionary even defines despair by contrasting it to our understanding of hope. The Oxford Dictionary explains despair as "the complete loss or absence of hope" or (as a verb) to "lose or be without hope."[24] The Cambridge English Dictionary is more detailed. It defines despair as "the feeling that there is no hope and that you can do nothing to improve a difficult or worrying situation."[25]

Despair is so connected to hope its meaning hinges on the absence of hope.

Plainly put, despair is what we experience when hope is gone.

Like the bee, humans live in a world under attack. Predators, pests, pathogens, and poisons also attack our existence. There seems to be no shortage of threats to our physical and spiritual health.

Despair is an onslaught against our mind, body, and soul.

I think we are quite a lot like the honeybee on this level. We go about our day-to-day lives, performing our tasks, mostly unaware of the threats surrounding us. We assume the bridge will hold up as we drive across it during our daily commute. We trust the pilot knows how to fly the plane that we presume the engineers have designed safely. We believe the doctors can treat and give us the best medicine possible. We trust one another to stay in the proper traffic lane as we race head-on over the highways.

We place our hope in ourselves or in others all the time.

When this trust-filled hope is broken, when we are attacked, or if some calamity comes our way, we often experience despair. We can become traumatized. The loss of hope can pull us further from one another and likely away from God.

Just as a beekeeper does not set up a hive to create a buffet for ants, skunks, and bears, our God did not make the universe intending us to suffer as we do. No, our fallen state is the root of despair. We read about the birth of despair just a few short chapters forward from the perfect story of God's hope-filled creation. It is the story of man's fall.

Genesis 3 begins with the story of the enemy attacking God's idealistic creation.

> NOW THE SERPENT WAS MORE CRAFTY THAN ANY OTHER BEAST OF THE FIELD THAT THE LORD GOD HAD MADE. HE SAID TO THE WOMAN, "DID GOD ACTUALLY SAY, 'YOU SHALL NOT EAT OF ANY TREE IN THE GARDEN'?" [2] AND THE WOMAN SAID TO THE SERPENT, "WE MAY EAT OF THE FRUIT OF THE TREES IN THE GARDEN, [3] BUT GOD SAID, 'YOU SHALL NOT EAT OF THE FRUIT OF THE TREE THAT IS IN THE MIDST OF THE GARDEN, NEITHER SHALL YOU TOUCH IT, LEST YOU DIE.' " [4] BUT THE SERPENT SAID TO THE WOMAN, "YOU WILL NOT SURELY DIE. [5] FOR GOD KNOWS THAT WHEN YOU EAT OF IT YOUR EYES WILL BE OPENED, AND YOU WILL BE LIKE GOD, KNOWING GOOD AND EVIL." [6] SO WHEN THE WOMAN SAW THAT

> THE TREE WAS GOOD FOR FOOD, AND THAT IT WAS A DELIGHT TO THE EYES, AND THAT THE TREE WAS TO BE DESIRED TO MAKE ONE WISE, SHE TOOK OF ITS FRUIT AND ATE, AND SHE ALSO GAVE SOME TO HER HUSBAND WHO WAS WITH HER, AND HE ATE. [7] THEN THE EYES OF BOTH WERE OPENED, AND THEY KNEW THAT THEY WERE NAKED. AND THEY SEWED FIG LEAVES TOGETHER AND MADE THEMSELVES LOINCLOTHS.[26]

In the Genesis story, we see the enemy using deceit to destroy the perfect intent of God's creation. He tempts the created and accuses the Creator of trying to hide knowledge.

The resulting fall leads to the despairing evils of a fallen world.

Understanding the spiritual warfare at work by the enemy is important for guarding our hearts and minds against evil. We are wise to know our enemy and the ploys of the dark forces that attack us.

Sun Tzu, author of the ancient Chinese text: *The Art of War*, wisely stated:

> "If you know the enemy and know yourself, you need not fear the result of a hundred battles. If you know yourself but not the enemy, for every victory gained you will also suffer a defeat. If you know neither the enemy nor yourself, you will succumb in every battle."[27]

The Biblical account of the enemy gives us insight into knowing our enemy and his motivations. It teaches us to be on alert against attacks on any front. The writer of 1 Peter urges us to "[8] Be sober-minded; be watchful. Your adversary the devil prowls around like a roaring lion, seeking someone to devour."[28]

Like the numerous threats facing honeybees, our innermost beings face a plethora of challenges. Our spiritual enemy, seeking to cause despair, is on the attack.

He is everywhere.

In his classic book, *The Strategy of Satan: How to Detect and Defeat Him*, Warren Wiersbe summarizes the Biblical explanation of the evil one. He outlines how Satan acts as the:

- Deceiver
- Destroyer
- Tempter
- Accuser[29]

As the Deceiver, Satan attacks to make us ignorant of God's will. He lies to us and tricks us.

According to Wiersbe, the Destroyer wants to make us impatient with God's plan or His will. Our sin results in anger directed at God.

The Tempter then lures us to act independently of God's will. We become outrageously more rebellious and lawless. We go our own way.

Finally, in our desperate state of separation, the Accuser launches his final attack. He indicts us as guilty. The enemy knows God is just and holy, so the accuser needs only to rely on God's nature for sentencing.

In our sin, we are found guilty.

The final result of the enemy's tricks is to bring us to a sense of despair. Deceived, our actions lead to destruction. We are defeated and tempted to blame God for our state of demise. In our final state of hopelessness, we abandon faith and succumb as the Accuser deals his final blow.

What a desperate situation!

Thankfully, there is a plan to combat our despair and restore us to a fullness of hope.

6

Stages

It's dark, but the queen knows her way.

Slowly, she moves along the walls, following the contours of her home.

She is, of course, not alone.

She is never alone.

Her attendants surround her, anticipating every need.

Although little to no light reaches the dark, warm interior of her chamber, she senses the presence of the others. They guide her, feed her, and protect her.

Constant companions and helpers surround the queen.

Through the darkness, unseen, hidden, they move together.

They stay at her side. They guard her and keep her fed.

She feels safe.

The queen, solitary in her role, should feel entirely secure.

She is protected well inside a fortress, surrounded by her progeny.

After some searching, the queen lowers her swollen abdomen into the chamber prepared for her. She pauses for a moment to deposit a treasure. A single egg. "During peak season, a quality queen can lay over 3,000 eggs per day - that's more than her own body weight in eggs in a day!"[30] Some estimates put this at over 500,000 eggs throughout her lifecycle.

Over and over, the queen repeats the process of birthing eggs.

It is her purpose.

The queen determines the gender of each bee based on the needs of the colony. In doing so, she foretells the purpose of each of her offspring. A male to spread her progeny to other colonies, or a female to build, protect, steward, perhaps even take her place.

It's a girl!

Most honeybees will be female.

Because female bees do the lion's share of the work in a colony, laying a female egg is an optimistic look toward tomorrow. Each egg is born with a bit of hope.

As the egg is deposited gently in the dark, the queen leaves; her work with this child is completed. The nurse bees will take it from here. In the darkness of the hive, the queen moves from cradle to cradle, cementing the future of her hive with each egg.

The little bee deposited here in the darkness is smaller than a grain of rice. The child will quickly double, triple, and then quadruple in size within the coming weeks.

The nurse bees, her sisters, will bring just the right amount of food. "Every larva receives about 10,000 nurse bee feeding visits during development - this means that each larva is fed on average every 43 seconds!"[31]

She will grow from egg, to larva, to pupa, and after about 21 days, she will finally emerge as a fully mature, adult bee.[32]

Each bee moves through these four stages of development. The Honey Bee Research Centre, an organization that traces its origins all the way back to 1894 at the Ontario Agricultural College, explains the four stages of honeybee growth.

- "**Egg:** A queen will lay one egg per cell throughout the brood nest, which is located in the center of the hive. They are very small and look like grains of rice. Worker eggs are laid in smaller cells and drone eggs are laid in larger cells.
- **Larva:** After about 3 days, an egg will hatch into a larva. Worker bees will feed and tend to the larvae as they grow. Once the larva is big enough, the worker bees will cover their cell with a wax capping.
- **Pupa:** once the cell is capped, the larva will spin a cocoon around itself and develop into a pupa (similar to how a butterfly spins a chrysalis). At this stage, the baby bee develops its eyes, legs, wings and other familiar body parts.
- **Adult:** Finally, once the pupa is done growing it becomes an adult honey bee. When it is ready, the bee will begin to chew through the cocoon and wax capping of its cell and emerge into the hive."[33]

Over a few weeks, the tiny egg undergoes an incredible transformation. A female bee emerges, fully developed and ready to serve the needs of the colony.

She is born into a life of hopeful purpose.

When a honeybee first emerges, it immediately goes to work. It cleans its room.

Female bees perform different tasks based on their age. This "age-related division of labor" is called "temporal polyethism." In the simplest terms, it means the honeybee's role changes as she ages. Her work for the colony is based on a "somewhat predictable progression throughout her lifetime" and she does these age-assigned jobs "rather than specializing in a single task."[34]

Initially, worker bees work with the brood. The brood is a term used to describe the eggs, larvae or pupae of the colony and represents the future generation of the colony. Starting out, "young workers perform jobs in the central area of the hive where the brood is," and they focus on "cleaning brood cells, feeding and tending the brood, and tending to the queen."

Next, the aging worker bees "take on duties in the outer regions of the hive" that "include building comb, receiving nectar and pollen, storing nectar and pollen, processing honey and ventilating the hive." Finally, "the oldest bees perform tasks outside of the hive, such as guarding the hive, removing dead bees from the hive, and foraging."[35]

In each stage of life, the honeybee has a purpose uniquely fitted to its natural biology. In fact, "as she ages, different hormones in her body will increase and decrease." For example, "a decrease in vitellogenin protein and increase in" what is called "Juvenile Hormone" causes her body to make subtle transitions. The changes make her more adapted for moving "out of the hive" to take "up new tasks as a field bee, such as guarding and foraging."[36]

The more we study them, the greater our fascination with how incredibly these creatures are designed. Each bee goes through predictable stages and, importantly, each has a role in the community they call home.

For honeybees, their entire existence has intentionality.

They are born of hope and designed with purpose.

7

Beatitudes

Carved into the pristine coastal hills of Southern California sits one of America's wealthiest communities. La Jolla, meaning "the jewel" in Spanish, boasts posh boutiques and glamorous views of nature. The jagged rock walls, seals soaking in the sun, tide pools, and the constant sound of the surf combine to make it a true gem.

Some years ago, I was consulting for a church there. The Pastor, Adam, had asked me to help develop his family ministry plan. My daughter was with me, and Adam gave us a tour of his church.

My daughter seemed more interested in the pink, two-bedroom house on a corner across the road. Who could overlook such a beautiful home?

Did I mention it was pink?

Adam said to her, "You like that one? It's not a bad location, either. You could walk to my church, maybe we can hire you one day? That little house will probably only set you back two million dollars."

By the way, La Jolla is one of the most affluent zip codes in the USA. An article on Forbes.com, dated from around the time of our visit, placed La Jolla in the top 100 most expensive zip codes in America.[37]

Later that day, we were driving up the coast with our hosts.

I noted a beautiful apartment building on the cliff above the highway. It was elegantly perched atop a hill and overlooked the grandeur of the coastal valley. Porches and private decks surrounded the western side of the facility. Mirrored glass windows looked out across the majesty of the Pacific Ocean. I wondered about the cost of rent for such a place, gestured to it, and asked my friend what he knew about living there as he navigated the winding roads along the coast.

Adam explained to me I was not looking at a simple apartment building. It was a retirement community and quite prestigious. He said people save up their entire lives to move there. He didn't know the costs, but he suggested it was probably not in the cards for either of us as pastors.

I imagined, for a moment, retirement in such a place. Every cloudless evening, you would witness the most spectacular sunsets.

"The views must be amazing from up there?" I said to Adam.

He nodded in agreement. Then, he told me how he had visited someone from his church, a resident there.

He said, "The views are amazing and the place is luxurious. However, the residents often close the curtains and don't even notice the sunsets in the evening."

He gave me a side glance as he continued. "The sun's brightness keeps them from enjoying the evening news or their re-runs of old sit-coms."

I was stunned.

Can you imagine?

People worked their whole lives to live in this fantastic place. They move in and have this glamorous view of the sunset over the Pacific each evening. Over the years, they sacrificed and fought tooth and nail to earn enough money to retire in comfort and style. Perhaps they romantically envisioned, as I did, spending their twilight years holding the hands of someone they love as the sun, literally and proverbially, sinks over the horizon.

Yet, once they arrived in this coveted place, they chose to pull the blinds. The searing light was too brilliant for their dimmed eyes. It blinded them in its glory.

Instead, they rewatched episodes of "I Love Lucy" or "MASH."

This analogy aptly describes our American ideals of retirement. For most, although they may not admit it, retirement feels like a bit of a bait and switch.

People work hard to achieve the nirvana of retirement, only to find their health has given out. The things they once enjoyed are no longer an option due to mobility limitations.

Their family has grown up and moved away. The person they imagined holding hands with and lovingly spending their last moments together has preceded them in death.

In some cases, broken relationships have even left them estranged from those they once cared for.

Life is hard.

It often gets more difficult as we age.

The wear and tear of our youth pulls us closer to the grave. Sometimes, we buy into a common lie to distract ourselves from the challenges. We tell ourselves things will get easier with wealth.

We put our hope in the things of this world.

We say to ourselves, "If we could only retire in a place where people wait on us hand and foot as we watch the sunset over the Pacific each glorious evening."

For those of you who are younger, this bodes as a cautionary tale.

Remember to prepare yourselves for eternal retirement. Do not attempt to build the narcissistic vision of retirement our world tries to sell. Self-centered ideals of personal luxury often require us to sacrifice too much in the present. As we pursue those worldly hopes, we often discard the importance of our present relationships. We exchange love or time with loved ones, hoping for a far-off, imagined future.

We pursue a future life worth living instead of a present joy-filled contentment.

Our world places hope in hopeless things.

Life

If this disappointing look at retirement leaves you grasping for something to look forward to, then it is worth pausing to do a little self-reflection.

What does a life well-lived look like?

More simply asked, what is "the good life?"

In the mirror, we might even ask, is the life I'm building worth living?

Hope placed in the wrong thing, or things, creates all sorts of problems for us.

The future is not always going to be nice and easy.

So many people I know have worked all of their lives to build up a retirement fund. Once they met their goals, they sat in a chair, watched TV, or drank their lives away. They became miserable and detached from the world. They grew embittered during a season when their children and grandchildren needed their wisdom and love.

Each had a vision for a life worth living in their now-distant past versions of themselves. They had once hoped for a better tomorrow. For those who became most disillusioned, their imagined future was molded by self-centered desires.

Their hope was not rooted in something eternal or in helping others. It was not rooted in God's hope for them.

Luke

Jesus, in Luke chapter 6, challenges us to find our purpose. His message is counter-culture to the American ideals of self-indulgent retirement.

Christ casts a vision of a life lived with hope in the right things by contrasting misplaced hopes.

The Beatitudes offer a glimpse at what God would consider "a life worth living" through compare and contrast. These words, taken from Jesus' Sermon on the Plateau (or Mount), are among His most well-known.

They are often misunderstood and taken out of context.

To help us understand Jesus' teachings, as recorded by the Apostle Luke, we gain some insight by first exploring the author of this historical account of Christ. The Gospel of Luke was written to a non-Jewish, or Gentile, audience. Luke himself was not Jewish. He was not a member of the nation of God's chosen people.

Luke was a convert.

Despite his status as an outsider, Luke had come to know Jesus and had chosen to follow Him. It was not a birthright as much as it was a decision.

We can gain much from taking a perspective on Luke's work with consideration from his intended audience. In many ways, the Roman world in which Luke was writing was not too unlike our current world today.

The Romans, for example, were polytheistic. They believed and tolerated the belief of many gods across their empire.

Thus, Luke proclaims the one true God, Jesus Christ, in his writings. His explanations of Christ's works help us see the contrast between superstitious or legalistic religion and God's truth.

An obsession with power is another way the Romans were similar to our modern world. Romans were power-hungry & patriarchal (controlled by men). For Rome, power was a weapon wielded to control and subjugate others. Power determined one's influence and power was why only men, born as citizens and heirs to land, were given the authority to rule.

Generally speaking, seen as less than and weak, women, children, and enslaved people were all lumped together. They had little to no influence because they possessed no power.

In the Roman world, those who owned nothing were worthy of no honor.

Luke, by contrast, demonstrates the value of everyone, even the unborn, as he writes about the life of Jesus.

Greed is a third way modern America is similar to Rome. Money held extraordinary power in the Roman world. It is an obvious indicator of one's wealth, and money allows one to buy services and luxuries. Wealth brought the privilege of protection.

In ancient Rome, like today, affluence was esteemed. This often led to corruption and abuse. Money could buy citizenship.[38] Bribes swayed justice. Power and conquest permitted the elite to prosper, often at the expense of those who had less.

Into this world, Luke brings to our attention the words of Jesus. He reports on Jesus' teachings in ways difficult for those who struggle with greed. In Luke's two books, the Gospel bearing his name and the Book of Acts, we often see the contrasting of haves with the have-nots. Luke brings to light the conflict in a world divided between insiders and outsiders. Inescapable is the tension between the powerful and the powerless.

These comparisons make Luke's writings come to life.

It is why I love the Book of Luke.

He is writing to a Roman audience and speaks directly to the heart of many relevant challenges we, as Westerners, have inherited from ancient

Rome. There are numerous apparent parallels and applications for our modern world that we can draw from ancient Rome.

As some historians have noted, America is a type of new Rome.

Yes, that's both good and bad. We are the leading nation in terms of influence and strength. Our cultural impact directly or indirectly influences much of the world—the power we wield and the cultural values we exert are not unlike the prowess of ancient Rome.

Today, as the influence of Christianity wanes under the shifting tides of an increasingly secular culture, the US is becoming more and more like the ancient people to whom Jesus preached God's truth.

"Truth," in the land of the free, is relative.

This challenge, in part, is why it is an inspiring time to stand up and live your life for Christ.

As we will see, He presents us with a revolutionary, counter-cultural way of living!

So, what are the values Jesus so convincingly explained to His followers? How can they turn this broken world, filled with despair, back to a way of hope?

The Beatitudes

Yes, I did resist the temptation to write "BEE-attitudes" in a book using bees to teach us about hope.

You're welcome.

What are The Beatitudes?

The Beatitudes summarize Jesus' rebellious way of living. They are His TedTalk addressing life with God.

Jesus taught this message of counter-cultural love often enough that His disciples could recite it from memory years after Jesus' death and ascension. As proof of this, we read a version of Jesus' message recorded in two books of the Bible.

The Beatitudes appear in both the Books of Matthew and Luke.

Luke's version of Jesus' beatitudes uses compare and contrast to emphasize the point.

To help us highlight these contrasts, I will rearrange the beatitudes to highlight the parallel messages. Each statement in verses 24 through 26 opposes the ones presented first in verses 20 to 23.

Rich v. Poor

Starting with Luke 6:20 and verse 24. We see a contrast between rich and poor.

> [20] LOOKING AT HIS DISCIPLES, [JESUS] SAID:
> "BLESSED ARE YOU WHO ARE POOR,
> FOR YOURS IS THE KINGDOM OF GOD.[39]

Then, in verse 24, we read the counter statement.

> [24] "BUT WOE TO YOU WHO ARE RICH,
> FOR YOU HAVE ALREADY RECEIVED YOUR COMFORT.[40]

For the sake of clarification, the word blessed "refers to the distinctive religious joy" that comes from experiencing the salvation or saving grace of God.[41]

The Greek word translated here as "poor," is ptochoi (pe-toy-choy-e). Ptochoi "implies those who are utterly dependent on God" and rely on His provision for every need.[42] Their physical lack of wealth has created an environment where they must rely on God to get through each day in the most literal sense.

In their desperate poverty, hope points them to seek a God who provides.

We can imagine Jesus, the son of a humble carpenter, growing up as a poor commoner in a small village. He would have had a deep understanding of life driven by scarcity. As a child, Jesus would have witnessed desperation, and would have seen its consequences lived out daily in the lives of those around him. Impoverishment was the norm for many living in Israel under the occupation of the Romans.[43]

Contrary to the hopeful message for the poor, the rich receive caution. The warning for the rich is not just because they are wealthy; it is not classism. The original Greek word translated as rich is plousios, (ploo'-see-os) and means "having abundant possessions" or "abounding with" wealth.[44][45] It's use here implies the wealthy "have chosen present gratification over future blessing," and that they have a, "disregard for spiritual realities."[46] Remember, in Roman culture, it is even possible they have become rich at the expense of others' suffering.[47]

Affluence can be a stumbling block for many as it relates to power. The broader context of wealth coupled with power implies not just material comfort. It could be position, skills, relationships, influence, etc. The danger is receiving present satisfaction from something given a higher value than God.

Contrasting the physically poor with the worldly rich helps us see Jesus' meaning. Those who are rich in their need for God and in their distinctive joy from receiving His perfect salvation will be comforted. They are blessed because they know this world is not all they have.

They have placed hope in something eternal.

Therefore, when Jesus says, "But woe to you who are rich, for you have already received your comfort,"[48] He makes it clear the removal of material blessings leads to despair.

Hope is easily lost when it has been misplaced.

Temporary v. Eternal

Continuing through the Beatitudes, Jesus' powerful teaching deepens as we examine the next two verses and how they contrast one another. In verses 21 and 25, we see the difference between those who are hungry with those how are satisfied. They are compared alongside mourning and laughing. The jarring comparison shows our status in God's Kingdom is permanent and eternal. It is not a temporary fulfillment.

Verse 21 says:

> [21] BLESSED ARE YOU WHO HUNGER NOW,
> FOR YOU WILL BE SATISFIED.
> BLESSED ARE YOU WHO WEEP NOW,
> FOR YOU WILL LAUGH.[49]

Verse 25 contrasts these blessings with a warning.

> ²⁵ WOE TO YOU WHO ARE WELL FED NOW,
> FOR YOU WILL GO HUNGRY.
> WOE TO YOU WHO LAUGH NOW,
> FOR YOU WILL MOURN AND WEEP.⁵⁰

Undoubtedly, being satisfied with food and laughter are both temporary, non-permanent experiences. They are fleeting moments.

As taught by Jesus, hunger is a desperate reality. A lack of food is a harsh recurring experience faced by people in poverty. Many of the outcasts who followed Jesus personally understood the pangs of an empty stomach. Luke's writing leans into this physical meaning of hunger to provide a spiritual truth.

If we look at the parallel record of Jesus' message in Matthew's Gospel, we see that, "hunger," could also carry the connotation of, "hungering for righteousness." Through this lens, the comparison of a spiritual hunger is more plainly stated.

Matthew 5:6 says:

> ⁶ BLESSED ARE THOSE WHO HUNGER AND
> THIRST FOR RIGHTEOUSNESS,
> FOR THEY WILL BE FILLED.⁵¹

We can draw even deeper understanding by considering the culture of the times. For instance, we could contrast the gluttonous feasts held by the Roman elites to the hunger experienced by people living in poverty.

The Romans would dine late into the evening in hours-long banquets of increasingly bizarre buffets. It was unchecked hedonism. Participating in each course of the spectacle was customary. As a result, some developed the practice of leaving "the table to vomit in a room close to the dining hall."[52] "They would use "a feather" to "tickle the back of their throats to stimulate the urge to regurgitate."[53] Pressure relieved from their gut, they then returned to the orgy of dining experiences.

What Jesus is highlighting for us is the contrast of temporary satisfaction with the eternal. The impermanent satisfaction we experience in this world will never truly satisfy the deepest part of our soul.

Like a glutton, we will always want for more. Unsatisfied, the world leaves us hoping for the next experience and despairing when we find ourselves hungering for more temporary satisfaction, no matter how thrilling it is in the moment.

The contrast seen in verses 21 and 25 teaches us not to place our hope in the treasures of this world. Rather, we find blessings when we learn to hunger for God's righteousness.

According to Jesus, those who hunger deeply for God experience a distinctive joy from receiving His salvation. Those who fill themselves with the wisdom or materials of this world are always wanting.

The temporary will never satisfy eternally.

During the weeks leading up to Easter, many practice some form of fasting. Fasting is a spiritual discipline that reminds us to only hunger for God's righteousness. If gluttony is a struggle, I challenge you to participate in fasting.[54] Give something up and when you want it, pray through this passage of scripture from the Beatitudes. It will bless you as you find your hope in Jesus and not in satisfying a physical, emotional, or sexual appetite.

Before we move on to the next comparison, we should also mention how mourning is contrasted with laughing in these verses. The Old

Testament story of Nehemiah sheds light on the meaning. In Nehemiah, we read about the people mourning when they realized they had neglected God's word. Then, as they stood to hear God's Word read aloud, they were moved to repentance. Their renewed knowledge of God's hope-filled promises allowed them to celebrate sincerely.

They rediscovered their joy-filled, hope in salvation by rediscovering God's truth.

Hope was re-born from their mourning!

By contrast, those who never take stock in their present lives, those who say "Yeah, I'm good on my own..." and can see no fault in their way, are the people to whom Jesus says, "Woe to you..." It seems the prophetic words of Jesus foretell the mourning and weeping destined for those who do not stop to get their lives in line.

In both the darkness of mourning and a hunger for something better, the believer can have hope for a better tomorrow.

We can have hope in desperate times, because we have an eternal hope in Jesus Christ.

Hated v. Loved

Finally, the last part of Luke's version of Jesus' Beatitudes compares hate with love. We read verses 22 to 23 in contrast with verse 26. Here, the comparison shows us the difference between being hated for the wrong reasons and being loved for not taking a stand.

Verse 22-23 tells us:

> [22] BLESSED ARE YOU WHEN PEOPLE HATE YOU,
> WHEN THEY EXCLUDE YOU AND INSULT YOU

> AND REJECT YOUR NAME AS EVIL,
> BECAUSE OF THE SON OF MAN.[55]
> ²³ "REJOICE IN THAT DAY AND LEAP FOR JOY,
> BECAUSE GREAT IS YOUR REWARD IN HEAVEN.
> FOR THAT IS HOW THEIR ANCESTORS TREATED THE PROPHETS.

Then, verse 26 gives the warning from Jesus.

> ²⁶ WOE TO YOU WHEN EVERYONE SPEAKS WELL OF YOU,
> FOR THAT IS HOW THEIR ANCESTORS
> TREATED THE FALSE PROPHETS.[56]

Well, what are we to do with that?

Is Jesus saying that we should pursue living in a manner in which we are to be hated? Do we only experience joy in our salvation when people hate us? Does it mean we are to try and present ourselves as martyrs?

Should we pick fights to show our faithfulness?

No, no, no, and no.

The Expositor's Commentary, a mainstay in many Seminary libraries, helps shed light on this passage. It says, "Luke is emphasizing the vindication (or victory) of God's people who patiently wait for Him."[57]

Our hope, founded in faith, is tightly connected to Jesus' victory over the world.

This is also a theme Jesus presents in His other teachings. In Luke 18, we see one such an example in the parable of the Persistent Widow.

> ¹ THEN JESUS TOLD HIS DISCIPLES A PARABLE TO SHOW THEM THAT THEY SHOULD ALWAYS PRAY AND NOT GIVE UP. ² HE SAID: "IN A CERTAIN TOWN THERE WAS A JUDGE WHO NEITHER FEARED GOD NOR CARED WHAT PEOPLE THOUGHT. ³ AND THERE WAS A WIDOW IN THAT TOWN WHO KEPT COMING TO HIM WITH THE PLEA, 'GRANT ME JUSTICE AGAINST MY ADVERSARY.'
> ⁴ "FOR SOME TIME HE REFUSED. BUT FINALLY HE SAID TO HIMSELF, 'EVEN THOUGH I DON'T FEAR GOD OR CARE WHAT PEOPLE THINK, ⁵ YET BECAUSE THIS WIDOW KEEPS BOTHERING ME, I WILL SEE THAT SHE GETS JUSTICE, SO THAT SHE WON'T EVENTUALLY COME AND ATTACK ME!' "
> ⁶ AND THE LORD SAID, "LISTEN TO WHE UNJUST JUDGE SAYS. ⁷ AND WILL NOT GOD BRING ABOUT JUSTICE FOR HIS CHOSEN ONES, WHO CRY OUT TO HIM DAY AND NIGHT? WILL HE KEEP PUTTING THEM OFF? ⁸ I TELL YOU, HE WILL SEE THAT THEY GET JUSTICE, AND QUICKLY. HOWEVER, WHEN THE SON OF MAN COMES, WILL HE FIND FAITH ON THE EARTH?"[58]

One lesson we can draw from this parable is faithfulness despite persecution.

A bad judge corrupts justice, yet he does the right thing in response to someone's persistence. Therefore, we can find hope in asking, "How much more will our God, who is absolutely just and loving, do the right thing?"

Jesus challenges us to remember God will be victorious. When we remember God's goodness in our daily routines, we live a life worth living. We have hope for a better day.

As followers of Christ, therefore, we must ensure to chase the right things. We don't go out looking for a theological fight or judging those we have no relationship with. Our hope should be in pursuing God. Otherwise, we are going the wrong way altogether.

I had a friend in middle school who, like me, sat on the bench for the basketball team. He was a great guy. Neither one of us was a great basketball player.

One time, my friend got put into the game during the last quarter. Benchwarmers normally got an opportunity to play in those final moments of the game. Either we were too far behind to hope for a comeback, or we were far enough ahead that the coach felt we couldn't mess it up too much. It was generally the former and hardly the latter.

When my friend got put into the game, someone immediately passed him the ball. With the court wide open, he looked up and realized that this was his moment.

He made a fast break.

Dribbling frantically, just as we had practiced over and over again, he made a straight line, completely uncontested. He took a calculated final step, confidently tossed the ball against the backboard, and sank a flawless layup.

As he turned to celebrate, fists pumping the air, he heard everyone cheering him on.

Then, a sickening realization struck him. He looked toward his teammates and the coach. It was then he realized the crowd had not been cheering his success. Nope. In fact, they were now yelling or laughing.

He had just scored for the opposing team.

The coach, either frustrated or despairing, dropped his head into his hands. A few moments later, we were so far behind that he put me in the game.

Like many people with misplaced faith, my friend thought he was doing the right thing. His misguided efforts ended up scoring for the opposing team.

How often do well-meaning people only complicate things by going with the crowd?

Perhaps this hints at Jesus' more profound teachings on unity and love. Ultimately, we are challenged by Jesus' Beatitudes to not get to the end of our lives, only to realize we have been scoring for the wrong team all along.

Being the Beatitudes

Self-examination is an excellent place to start any serious Bible study. It becomes essential when we try to apply Jesus' challenging words to our modern lives.

We could begin by asking ourselves, "What am I rich in that separates me from God?"

The first thing entering our mind from this question will probably be the most telling. For example, if you immediately think of the balance in your bank accounts or the value of your investment portfolio, I think Jesus has a word of caution for you to consider.

Our culture gets excited about money and wealth. Remember, we have that in common with our Roman ancestors. Yet, God's Kingdom doesn't run on our private sense of affluence.

Practicing generosity is a healthy discipline we can use to free our hearts from the traps of greed. As we grow more intentional in our giving, it equips the Church and other nonprofits to serve the local community. Our gifts provide for those in need. In the Church, we tithe as a means of worship. God's economy does not operate on scarcity. I would advise not to let money get in the way of what Jesus is trying to teach us here.

Richness in money is not what the Beatitudes are about.

No.

It is the relationship, person, position, wealth, or things we have placed value upon that Jeus is warning us against. It is the danger of valuing something greater than our relationship with God. Jesus is calling us to make Him the center of our everything.

Jesus urges us to release whatever we are holing onto in our hearts and to be found completely in Him. The resulting freedom is key to growing to be like Jesus.

Walking in the Way of Jesus, placing our hope only in God; this is the point of the Beatitudes. Being like Jesus is being the beatitudes.

We become hope born into action.

Therefore, in our moments of self-examination, we ask "What am I rich in that separates me from God?"

Have you put your hope in the wealth you have stored?

Have you hope in the strength of your hands?

Have you put hope in your relationships or your family's good name?

Maybe you have worked hard your entire life. Maybe you have been promoted to a position of great influence or established a successful business. Maybe you are trusting in your charm and good looks.

All of those things are good on their own. Yet, when our faith becomes rooted, and our hope is founded on earthly things rather than in God, Jesus says, "Woe to you."

By contrast, Jesus' Beatitudes challenge us to examine our hearts and ask:

- What are you hungry for that draws you nearer to God?
- What is it that you are lacking?
- What do you most desire?
- Is it a material thing that consumes your thoughts?
    - Greed?
    - Gluttony?
    - Power?
    - Lust?

We can all relate to these challenging temptations. Freeing ourselves from their trap is worth the effort.

When I was younger, I wanted a motorcycle so much it was all I could think of. My wife will tell you, I was obsessed. Every spring I'd get the itch and start talking about the latest motorcycle I HAD to have!

There is nothing wrong with wanting a new Harley Davidson. It is when that desire becomes a driving factor for your every waking thought. It is when wanting something, whatever it may be, supplants God in our hearts. That's the danger.

From Jesus, we learn to examine our future hopes and the inner desires of our hearts. He shows us that what we crave is often connected to what we want. However, it is seldom what we need.

As we use the Beatitudes for self-examination, our inner truth is exposed.

What does it look like if we turn our material desires into a more profound and more urgent need for God?

What if God's love, mercy, and righteousness replaced the material things you hungered for?

How would it change you?

How would it impact your family?

How would it transform your community, even our world?

For most, pursuing such a radical love is nothing short of revolutionary.

When we choose to hope in a more profound knowledge of God instead of our selfish desires, we discover an eternal sense of "the good-life." Our life is filled with joy and temporary challenges, although still hard, fall away in the light of God's perfect hope.

In the words of Jesus, we are blessed.

From this blessing, He then challenges us to share His hope with others!

8

Swarm

Swarm season is a uniquely exciting time for beekeepers.

Honeybees begin to dramatically grow in number as winter thaws and gives way to warmer spring air.

As their numbers increase beyond the capacity of their home, the colony will prepare to split.[59] This process is called "swarming," and it is "the natural mode of reproduction for a honey bee colony."[60]

An article by the Tennessee Department of Agriculture explains it this way:

> "SWARMING IS INDUCED AS BEES INCREASE THEIR POPULATION SIZE AND REQUIRE MORE SPACE. A SWARM USUALLY CONSISTS OF THE OLD QUEEN (SOMETIMES A NEW ONE) AND 50 TO 60% OF THE WORKER BEES IN THE SWARMING COLONY. WORKERS PREPARING TO SWARM ENGORGE THEMSELVES ON HONEY AND FORCE THE OLD QUEEN OUT OF THE HIVE. CHANGING WEATHER CONDITIONS FROM COOL/RAINY TO WARM/SUNNY SEEM TO STIMULATE THE NATURAL URGE OF BEES TO SWARM."[61]

When the bees do move, they move en masse.

One year, early in the summer, I checked on our chickens and peacocks. The birds live near the apiary. In the distance, I could hear a faint hum in the air. It was louder than the typical buzz of the bees.

It got my attention and piqued my curiosity.

As I started to walk West towards the bee yard, the sound got louder and louder. Then, as my eyes began to focus on the cloud moving towards me, I realized what was happening.

One of my colonies was swarming.

Menacingly, the swarm was moving straight toward me. An ominous, black, amoebic cloud of thousands of honeybees was rapidly approaching.

Immediately, I started taking mental notes of what equipment I had available. I knew the bees would eventually land. If they stopped somewhere close by, I could catch them and move them into a hive box.

I had never seen a swarm on the move before. In a few short moments, an immense cloud of bees surrounded me.

They were everywhere.

I stood perfectly still and allowed them to pass.

The swarm moved past me, flying at about shoulder height. They seemed oblivious to my existence. In contrast to what you might expect, I was enthralled. I was overtaken with a mixture of fascination, curiosity, and awe.

First off, the sound was amazing! It was an indescribable experience I wanted to share with others. Once I had moved to a safe distance, I reached for my cell phone, hit record, and began to follow them.

Eventually, the bees landed on a tree near the garden.

I donned my bee suit, collected an empty hive box from the barn, and got ready to collect them. First, I put a large blanket under the branch where the bees were resting. Next, an empty box was put underneath them. Then, I gently gave the branch a downward shake. The colony fell into the box. Some of them took flight, others fell on the blanket.

As the day went on, the bees returned to the scent of their queen. She was in the box, surrounded by her family. I waited until dark so any stray foragers could return.

By sunset, all the bees return to the relative safety of their colony. I suited back up in the dark and grabbed a flashlight. Finally, after a long day of anticipation, I wrapped the equipment up to move it. Yes, the guard bees are still vigilant at night. I cautiously put the newly formed colony in an open spot at our apiary.

The bees were home. I was exhausted. I like to think we were all happy.

Reproduction

Collecting bee swarms benefits both the beekeeper and the bees. Providing a safe place for the bees to call home protects the colony from predation. At the same time, it is a natural way to expand honey production efforts.

Although it is an alarming thing to witness, the swarming process is a natural part of the reproductive cycle of honeybees. Of course, if a colony is going to split, and there is only one queen per colony, they have to make a new queen.

To accomplish this, "the workers build special wax cells" around a female egg and feed her only royal jelly.[62] "Royal jelly is composed of approximately two-thirds water, one-eighth proteins, 11 percent simple sugars, small quantities of Vitamin C and various trace minerals and enzymes."[63]

Previously, it was thought the exclusivity of only feeding a female worker bee the royal jelly would result in the formation of a queen. However, new research suggests queen formation may be a result of what they are not fed. Worker bees are fed some royal jelly and also bee bread. Bee bread is "pollen mixed with bee saliva and flower nectar" and is another food product the bees create "inside the honeycomb cells of a hive."[64] Withholding the "honey and beebread deliberately" from future queens, and because these products are "added by nurses to worker jelly," results in a type of chemical castration for the workers.[65]

Regardless of the exact details of how they form, the "new queen will then inherit her mom's old house, and take over the duties of laying eggs."[66] It is "the original, older queen" who will flee the hive, and as she does, she "will take half of the workers and leave the nest."[67]

The majestic cloud of intimidation, known as a honeybee swarm, is nothing more than an usurped "old queen and some of her workers looking for a new home."[68] The loyal host of bees will move to a new location and huddle together to protect their matriarch. Once the scout bees have found a safe place to call home, they will move as a single unit to set up shop and establish the new colony.[69]

Back in the original colony, the virgin queen will quickly move to eliminate any unhatched competitors. If necessary, when two or more queens hatch at once, they will fight for domination. It is most likely a fight to the death.

When she has established dominance, the new queen will depart the colony for a series of mating flights. The "queen can mate several times during a single flight," and she will often perform several consecutive nuptial flights on the same day or on different days."[70] The queen makes the most of her in-flight time by releasing a pheromone to attract mates. "The number of drones (male honeybees) a queen mates with ranges between 6 and 26," with most queens having "an average of 12–14."[71] The mating process will kill each successful male.

The queen will spend the rest of her life with her progeny. She won't leave the hive again until a new queen eventually replaces her. Every egg she ever produces will result from her initial mating flight.

The swarming process and the queen's mating flight create a legacy by establishing a new colony of honeybees.

9

Legacy

When I was serving as a missionary and training local churches, I traveled often. I've been to five of the seven continents. I've visited all 6 states in Australia and almost all 50 of the United States. Altogether, I have touched down in about 40 different countries and have experienced almost every climate our planet offers.

When my family and I lived in Louisville, we were fifteen minutes from the airport. My kids would hear my stories of where I had been and tell me places they wanted to go. And because we live in an era where travel is easy, I'd say to them the same thing over and over.

"Go. You should go see that place."

Then, one of the kids would say, "But it's so far away."

I'd reply, "Look, you can be anywhere on the planet with a 15-minute drive and a one or two-mile walk."

When they gave me a puzzled look, I'd lay out the itinerary:

- All you have to do is drive to the airport and walk to the plane.
- At the proper time, you find your seat and buckle up.
- People will bring you food and drinks.

- Maybe you watch a movie, read a book, or take a nap.
- When you land, you might have to walk to another airplane.
- Again, you sit, wait, watch movies, eat, sleep, take off, land, walk a little more, and on and on.

Before you know it, you are on an entirely different part of the planet. All you had to do to get there was decide to go.

Travel in our modern era is easier than ever before. It's not like we must take a wagon train to the nearest port city and travel for months just to cross the ocean. No, we've got air conditioning and Netflix, and, importantly, we can fly.

It is so easy to go. I used to measure the length of my trips by how many feature-length films I could watch. Belize, for example, is only one or two movies and a nap away. By contrast, heading down under to Australia is four to six movies and two or three attempts to nap.

Those long trips are rough but, historically speaking, quite simple.

Ok, so why am I talking about travel?

Church

The Book of Acts includes a lot of difficult travel. It is both geographic and spiritual travel. The story, written by the Apostle Luke, begins in Jerusalem with the ascension of Jesus and the Great Commission. By the end of the book, Paul, a man formerly hell-bent on destroying Christianity, is its biggest advocate and proclaiming the faith in Rome.

When we think about a faith legacy, what is passed on from generation to generation, it is helpful to consider how the Church came into existence. Luke's Book of Acts tells the story for us. In Acts, we discover how our legacy of faith was launched from the early Church.

Likewise, the study of Church history is an inquiry into the legacy of Christianity. It helps us understand the basics of our faith. Because each generation and era passes down traditions about how we practice our faith, studying the origin helps us ensure we are continuing in the same path of hope from the beginning.

Ultimately, knowing our history strengthens our hope and helps us discover what our part is in God's Kingdom.

The Book of Acts, coupled with Paul's letters, are full of legacy-building traditions to guide worshippers in any era. They tell the story of the early Church's formation. Collectively, these scriptures of the New Testament also paint an inspirational picture of what the Church should be like today.

Paul and the other apostles paint a picture of a unity built on hope. It is their legacy, put down in writing and handed down over the centuries, that defines our idea of what it means to be the Church.

In my experience, participating in a local church is about transformation. It is a move from individuality to community. Understanding this process requires each member to change.

Together, we all agree to submit ourselves to God's reign. We die to our self-centered ideals. Then, assuming the church is truly centered on Jesus' teachings, we grow to become more like Him as we serve one another in love.

Jesus is the point of Church. It brings people to Him.

The Church is His legacy.

Transformation, or spiritual movement, is required to grow in the way of Jesus. It is a commitment to transformation. Paul writes about this in Romans 12:1-2.

> THEREFORE, I URGE YOU, BROTHERS AND SISTERS, IN VIEW OF GOD'S MERCY, TO OFFER YOUR BODIES AS A LIVING SACRIFICE, HOLY AND PLEASING TO GOD—THIS IS YOUR TRUE AND PROPER WORSHIP. ² DO NOT CONFORM TO THE PATTERN OF THIS WORLD, BUT BE TRANSFORMED BY THE RENEWING OF YOUR MIND. THEN YOU WILL BE ABLE TO TEST AND APPROVE WHAT GOD'S WILL IS—HIS GOOD, PLEASING AND PERFECT WILL.[72]

When we as believers gather for church, it is a commitment to be changed. If we refuse to change and hinge our hope on traditions, it doesn't work. Together, we participate in an act of collective submission to Jesus and a rejection of the ways of this world.

In sincerity of faith, we reject manmade religion.

Gathering to focus on God, Church becomes an experience by which we grow closer to Him as one body.

This transformation does not happen accidentally. Spiritual change will only happen as we seek to offer ourselves to God through an intentional effort. It is how we become, in Paul's words "a living sacrifice, holy and pleasing to God." Transformed by the renewing of our minds, we can then test and approve what God's perfect and pleasing good will is in our homes, work, lives, and all things.

As we do, we too become a part of His legacy.

Adventure

I like to think of involvement in a local body of believers as an adventure. We are moving through time and space together. Existing and living with one another.

In thinking of our experiences together, the voice of J.R.R. Tolkien's character, Frodo Baggins, rings true. In *The Fellowship of the Ring*, Frodo remembers something his uncle, the adventurer Bilbo Baggins, used to say to him and he says:

> "... there was only one Road; that it was like a great river: its springs were at every doorstep and every path was its tributary. 'It's a dangerous business, Frodo, going out of your door,' he used to say. 'You step into the Road, and if you don't keep your feet, there is no telling where you might be swept off to.'"[73]

I think an optimistic and adventurous outlook at our daily challenges is a beautiful way to think of our journey through life. We are all connected to one great adventure. We are better solidified in unity then we are on our own. It is one solidary, not solitary, adventure.

We are part of a moment.

Each local church, therefore, is moving together. We are all connected to the Biblical narrative.

We might even think of the Bible differently through this adventure-tainted lens.

In the New Testament, for example, we can see the Gospels become the creation and Genesis story. The Book of Acts is the Exodus. It is the march of freedom and the move from bondage to the promised land. Finally, the Pauline letters are a type of law instructing us to live out God's love, similar to the stories of the kings and judges of old. Combined, they become a springboard from which we launch into the future.

We become a tangible extension of the Church the apostles established with Jesus.

Like a honeybee swarm, we replicate by building upon our past.

To think in this manner requires a subtle shift in our mindset. It requires change. Although change is more difficult for some than others, the fact remains: every church changes.

Everything that every church does now as part of a ceremonial tradition was, at some time or another, a new idea. It was an innovation; it required change.

If we survey all of the Church's history, no change has been as radical as what we read about in the Book of Acts. Luke's explanation of how the Church moved forward in the absence of Jesus after He ascended is a story of change and transformation. Therefore, Acts helps us to understand how change is necessary to reach our goal.

Change opens the door to becoming a church centered on Jesus Christ.

Change launches us into a legacy-building adventure of faith.

In his second letter to the church in Corinth, Paul writes about the purpose of our time in worship together. He makes it clear that we are to keep our focus on Jesus and not on ourselves. 2 Corinthians 4:5-6 tells us this:

> [5] FOR WHAT WE PREACH IS NOT OURSELVES, BUT JESUS CHRIST AS LORD, AND OURSELVES AS YOUR SERVANTS FOR JESUS SAKE. [6] FOR GOD, WHO SAID, "LET LIGHT SHINE OUT OF DARKNESS," MADE HIS LIGHT SHINE IN OUR HEARTS TO GIVE US THE LIGHT OF THE KNOWLEDGE OF GOD'S GLORY DISPLAYED IN THE FACE OF CHRIST.[74]

Understanding our purpose, to preach Jesus and not ourselves, helps us stay focused. We are continuing Jesus' legacy. We are proclaiming His light in a dark world. It is His glory that is displayed through us.

This is revolutionary, but it is not new. It is simply a continuation of what Jesus began.

It is His adventure-filled legacy of hope.

Acts

The Book of Acts begins where the gospels end.

Jesus proclaims, with His life, ministry, death, and resurrection, this loud message for all:

- You are worth the effort.
- You are worth the sacrifice.
- You are worth the price He paid.

To our God, you are the hill to die on. You are worth the fight.

Everything about Jesus gives us hope. Even the way He left.

In Acts, Luke records how Jesus' hope-giving life continued, after His exit, through the work of those who followed Him.

To understand this, let's look first at the end of Luke's Gospel. Luke 24:50-53 tells us about the Ascension of Jesus.

> [50] WHEN HE HAD LED THEM OUT TO THE VICINITY OF BETHANY, HE LIFTED UP HIS HANDS AND BLESSED THEM. [51] WHILE HE WAS BLESSING THEM, HE LEFT THEM AND WAS TAKEN UP INTO HEAVEN. [52] THEN THEY WORSHIPED HIM AND RETURNED TO JERUSALEM WITH GREAT JOY. [53] AND THEY STAYED CONTINUALLY AT THE TEMPLE, PRAISING GOD.[75]

Where Luke's first book ends, his second one (The Book of Acts) continues. Luke continues his historical and investigative report on Jesus from the same perspective. As Luke writes, we read about how the Church began.

Luke explains his purpose for writing in Luke 1 and Acts 1.

This is Luke 1.:1-4

> [1] MANY HAVE UNDERTAKEN TO DRAW UP AN ACCOUNT OF THE THINGS THAT HAVE BEEN FULFILLED AMONG US, [2] JUST AS THEY WERE HANDED DOWN TO US BY THOSE WHO FROM THE FIRST WERE EYEWITNESSES AND SERVANTS OF THE WORD. [3] WITH THIS IN MIND,

> **SINCE I MYSELF HAVE CAREFULLY INVESTIGATED EVERYTHING FROM THE BEGINNING, I TOO DECIDED TO WRITE AN ORDERLY ACCOUNT FOR YOU, MOST EXCELLENT THEOPHILUS, ⁴ SO THAT YOU MAY KNOW THE CERTAINTY OF THE THINGS YOU HAVE BEEN TAUGHT.**[76]

Now, just to connect the dots, let's look at Acts 1:1-2.

> **¹ IN MY FORMER BOOK, THEOPHILUS, I WROTE ABOUT ALL THAT JESUS BEGAN TO DO AND TO TEACH ² UNTIL THE DAY HE WAS TAKEN UP TO HEAVEN, AFTER GIVING INSTRUCTIONS THROUGH THE HOLY SPIRIT TO THE APOSTLES HE HAD CHOSEN.**[77]

You might note that Luke is addressing these two letters to the same person. Scholars pretty much agree this is not a specific person named "Theophilus," a name meaning "lover of God."[78] Rather, they think it is more of an open letter sent to someone who wants their true identity kept secret. The resulting ambiguity allows all to read Luke's letters as if they were personally written to us.

More importantly, we learn a lot by looking at the similarities of Luke's stated purpose.

Luke's Gospel gives "an account of the things that have been fulfilled among us..." The Book of Acts is a continuation of the former. Luke says, "¹In my former book, Theophilus, I wrote about all that Jesus began to do and to teach ² until the day he was taken up to heaven..."

Therefore, as we study the Book of Acts we need to look at it through the filter Luke uses. Acts, and all the Church ever does throughout history, is a continuation of "all that Jesus began to do and to teach."

It is so important to see this.

Luke says the purpose of Acts is to explain the continued work of Jesus. The Book of Acts is not just about Peter and Paul.

- Acts is not only a book about the historical origins of the Church.
- Acts is not only to chronicle the persecution of the early church fathers.
- Acts is not simply a book on theology; although we can learn some profound things about applying our faith, theology is also not the primary point.

The primary focus of the Book of Acts is Jesus Christ.

Jesus began a hope-filled legacy. It was reproduced, at great personal cost, through His people.

The Book of Acts continues to explain the work of Jesus Christ after His death and resurrection as His legacy lives on through His people.

This purpose is foundational for us to understand and to keep in mind as we continue to read into the intro of Acts.

Continuing in verse 3 of Acts 1:

> [3] AFTER HIS SUFFERING, HE PRESENTED HIMSELF TO THEM AND GAVE MANY CONVINCING PROOFS THAT HE WAS ALIVE. HE APPEARED TO THEM OVER A PERIOD OF FORTY DAYS AND SPOKE ABOUT THE KINGDOM OF GOD. [4] ON ONE OCCASION, WHILE HE WAS EATING WITH THEM, HE GAVE THEM THIS COMMAND:

> "DO NOT LEAVE JERUSALEM, BUT WAIT FOR THE GIFT MY FATHER PROMISED, WHICH YOU HAVE HEARD ME SPEAK ABOUT. [5] FOR JOHN BAPTIZED WITH WATER, BUT IN A FEW DAYS YOU WILL BE BAPTIZED WITH THE HOLY SPIRIT."[79]

Jesus suffers and dies, but He returns. Jesus appears to His disciples and teaches them about "the kingdom of God," He gives them instructions about the promise of the Holy Spirit, which is to come.

Jesus, even as He leaves, provides us a future hope.

Commission

In verse 6, Luke records Jesus' clarification about His intentions.

Those gathered are looking to an earthly kingdom as their hope. An earthly reign is the legacy they want. However, Jesus wants them to understand He has more in store for them than just what is at present.

> [6] THEN THEY GATHERED AROUND HIM AND ASKED HIM, "LORD, ARE YOU AT THIS TIME GOING TO RESTORE THE KINGDOM TO ISRAEL?" [7] HE SAID TO THEM: "IT IS NOT FOR YOU TO KNOW THE TIMES OR DATES THE FATHER HAS SET BY HIS OWN AUTHORITY. [8] BUT YOU WILL RECEIVE POWER WHEN THE HOLY SPIRIT COMES ON YOU; AND YOU WILL BE MY WITNESSES IN JERUSALEM, AND IN ALL JUDEA AND SAMARIA, AND TO THE ENDS OF THE EARTH."[80]

Jesus promises power from the Holy Spirit.

We dare not miss Jesus' challenge. He commands all believers to "be my witnesses." Jesus instructs us with His words; then, He tells us what to do with all He has taught us.[81]

Equipped with hope, we are to go.

The disciples are commanded to go first to "Jerusalem, and in all Judea and Samaria, and to the ends of the earth."[82]

I've always heard this explained in terms of geography. If that was Jesus' only intent, we could understand it as applicable to all places. It would mean, by extension, our command from Jesus is to be His witnesses:

- In Jerusalem, or the place of our current residence. It is our home. For me, this would be Georgetown, Indiana. It is the geographic location of my church and where me and my family live.
- Next, Jesus says to go to Judea. We might extend this to think of a broader region near where we live. For example, the county or city nearest us. Where I live, this would be the Louisville, Kentucky region. Locally, we call this area Kentuckiana. Louisville is bordered to the north by the Ohio River. This local name combines the communities nearest the city that are south (in Kentucky) and north (in Indiana). It is the broader region where my extended family lives, and I've spent over 25 years as a pastor.
- Jesus then commands His people to Samaria. Geographically, these are the slightly more distant areas surrounding the region of Judea. In context, for Jesus, it is a place more foreign in its customs and beliefs. Again, to use a local example, the region of Appalachia or the inner parts of the City of Louisville could be a substitute. It is a not-to-distant area with many different beliefs and customs. Jesus commands us to go to our neighbors who are unlike us.

- Finally, Jesus commands us to go to all the earth to witness to all the world. Jesus' command is, plainly put, a global call to action. In our modern time, these are the places we might go or send missionaries. It is also our witness to people we interact with in the online global community.

This geographic way of looking at the Great Commission helps us understand our calling to extend our faith beyond the horizon. However, perhaps an additional meaning of what Jesus says can be found in how people treated the disciples in each place Jesus named:[83]

- Jerusalem - the city where Christ was crucified. We are to be His witnesses despite the fear of death.
- Judea - the region where Jesus was rejected. We are to witness to others in the face of inevitable opposition.
- Samaria - the land where the disciples felt out of place. They began looking down their noses at the people living there. Their judgemental attitudes became a challenge to their ability to witness to the lost, outsiders, and those perceived as "less-than." Jesus says, go to them as well.
- The ends of the earth - Jesus challenges us to extend our efforts to serve those in places where we are genuinely foreign. We are to go to strangers. We are to witness to all.

Whether you read the Great Commission through this relational lens or through the geographic one mentioned before, both are incredibly powerful. They have the same meaning in terms of how we practice our faith.

Jesus' command urges us to start where we are and to go.

As we embrace His calling, we begin to follow and serve Jesus everywhere. Our legacy of faith begins in our homes. It goes with us to our schools and our work. Sharing our faith extends to our community, (the coffee shop, grocery line, sports game, etc.) and anywhere we might find ourselves.

The point of Jesus' Great Commission is that we are to be witnesses for him; everywhere and at all times, regardless of the circumstances. Importantly, we are to do it in partnership with His power and through the help of His Holy Spirit.

Remember, the key to understanding the Book of Acts is how it explains the story of God working in and through His people. Luke begins the Book of Acts by explaining he was writing "... about all that Jesus began to do and to teach..."[84]

Therefore, whatever we do as His followers is a continuation of the work Jesus began.

The Church becomes Jesus' legacy in action.

Advance

If you are concerned about what this means for us today, don't be overly worried. It was undoubtedly challenging for the disciples to wrap their heads around, just as it is for us today. Their inability to grasp Jesus' full meaning may be why they remain staring at the sky as Jesus leaves them in Acts 1:9.

> [9] AFTER HE SAID THIS, HE WAS TAKEN UP BEFORE THEIR VERY EYES, AND A CLOUD HID HIM FROM THEIR SIGHT. [10] THEY WERE LOOKING INTENTLY UP INTO THE SKY AS HE WAS GOING, WHEN SUDDENLY TWO MEN DRESSED IN WHITE STOOD BESIDE THEM. [11]

> "MEN OF GALILEE," THEY SAID, "WHY DO YOU STAND HERE LOOKING INTO THE SKY? THIS SAME JESUS, WHO HAS BEEN TAKEN FROM YOU INTO HEAVEN, WILL COME BACK IN THE SAME WAY YOU HAVE SEEN HIM GO INTO HEAVEN."[85]

After being given instructions, the disciples stand around, looking up. We can imagine how silly these people looked, wondering at the sky.

In an act of mercy, two men appear, two messengers from God. They prod them along and tell them, more or less, "Stop staring and get to work."

Move forward.

Advance.

We can feel a little bad for the recently abandoned believers. There is a sense of longing as the disciples are left to stare into the clouds. They are looking back at what has happened, hoping to return to how things used to be. They wanted Jesus with them, the way it had been.

Jesus, they must have prayed: "Come back now!"

"We want you back."

"We need you here."

There are some similarities to the Exodus story in this longing to go back, in the desire to return to what felt comfortable. In Exodus 16, we read about the people of Israel grumbling and desiring to return to Egypt. They were afraid of where their food would come from. They thought they might starve in the desert. Change crippled them. They doubted as fear paralyzed them.

What happens in the Exodus story?

Well, in this moment of longing to go back, God provides hope. He gives them daily sustenance through manna and quail. It is food delivered from heaven. In a tangible sense, God fed them hope to sustain them.

Their hope fulfilled became part of their legacy.

It is easy to see the similarities in Exodus and this moment in Acts chapter 1. Hopeless people are looking back. They are desperate to return to what they had.

Speaking into both moments of despair, God says, "I will help you."

But, in each case, the believers have to move.

God says, "Go, be changed, be transformed."

The Exodus story propels the people of God forward and toward the Promised Land where they became a great nation. In Acts, the challenge to advance into all nations becomes the Church's origin story.

It is our moment, just as it was the moment of the apostles.

Just like the apostles, we can get stuck with our eyes on the clouds if we are careless. We can miss opportunities to be witnesses of Jesus to our towns, to our counties, to our countries, and in our world.

We can retreat in fear from places hostile to the Lord. We can avoid sharing His love with people we think of as undeserving. But if we reject the calling, our legacy is despair.

If, by contrast, we accept our calling, we leave a legacy of hope for all generations.

Decide

You might ask, "How is it possible to create hope in a world filled with despair?"

Great question.

One way we can make a difference is to be open to change, especially in our local churches. It has been my experience that most changes are not optional. Change, or the complex choices we face, are most often forced upon us by the circumstances of our lives.

The most difficult changes occur when we lose people we care about. Changes like graduation, marriage, divorce, retirement, moving, and death are often out of our control. Loss is part of life.

These changes force us to figure out how to continue living, even when hardship is forced upon us.

Change requires courage and action in order to survive.

The necessary and involuntary nature of difficult change stretches everyone. To use the disciples' example, they stood around looking up at the clouds. The followers of Jesus were waiting for Him to come back before they could move. Change paralyzed them with inaction.

Jesus leaving was a change they did not ask for.

Thankfully, they persevered, and the fire lit within them transformed the entire world.

Can you imagine if they had never moved from that point?

Local churches and people of faith need to be open to change. More importantly, we need to be ready for change. We need to remember that even good change, like the freedom experienced by the formerly enslaved Israelites, can be challenging. Yet, our legacy of faith depends on an openness to change. We change for good and so that all may hear the good news of Jesus.

Good change is transformative and renewing.

It is a necessary tool for leaving a legacy of faith. Perhaps the best way to think about change, as a local church member, is to turn the mirror on ourselves. We each must allow ourselves to be transformed into the type of church we want to become.

Yes, God has challenged us to go to the ends of the earth. He has also called us to be focused on our own communities.

If you see something wrong with the world, with the church, or with your family, choose to leave a better legacy. Be an active part in the good type of change. Choose to be a part of what Jesus began. Then, as you seek to make your community a better reflection of Jesus, you, in turn, will change and be made new.

The result will be a legacy of hope for all generations to follow!

Step one is deciding you will be a part of the solution.

If you are reading this and have never decided to follow Jesus, what if you did that right now?

Join Jesus in His challenge to change the world for all people. Help your local church move forward. Commit to the best change anyone can ever make. Decide on a spiritual choice capable of transforming the trajectory of your eternal life.

Decide to follow Jesus.

When we choose Jesus, we begin to allow God to change us from the inside.

It starts when we receive or hear God's Word. You are doing that now by reading this.

Then, we choose to believe and act in faith. You are in control of this decision. God doesn't want you to be an automaton. He invites you to change; you decide.

We confess to God our need for forgiveness.

As we do, we turn from our old ways. We agree on our need for a savior. We reject the desires of our selfishness. We turn to God. The churchy word for turning to God is "repent." The Bible teaches that repenting is a moment of conversion.

It is when the old is gone, and the new has come.

We reject the world and follow Jesus.

In the New Testament, people who decided to follow Jesus were baptized as a means of a public confession of their faith. It was a shared moment to welcome the Holy Spirit into their lives.

We don't have to be legalistic about it, but baptism is a part of what the Apostles taught. We see it throughout the Book of Acts as a public declaration of faith.

If you are here, still reading, and this is you, **take the step of baptism and place your membership at a local church to grow in your faith.**

Decide for change now and unleash the hope of a love-filled legacy into your life today!

MICHAEL J. CHANLEY

Call or text me if you need help or have questions about this decision. My cell phone number is 650.636.7780 and, I hope to hear from you!

10

Superorganism

The first time I inspected my bee hives, I had one goal: to find the queen.

I carefully used my hive tool to pry up the outer cover. It made an audible pop as the propolis, a sticky substance bees produce to seal gaps, broke free.[86] As I gently lifted the top, I gave a couple of puffs of smoke from my bee-smoker. Immediately, the hive calmed down, and most of the guard bees retreated into the box.

Placing the lid out of the way, I carefully lifted the first frame. My senses came to life as I experienced the overwhelmingly delightful smell of a working beehive for the first time. The persistent buzz and the beautiful way light shimmered through the comb hooked me from the start.

As a novice, I didn't understand what I was looking at; it was a new experience. There were wax capped cells and a lot of activity. In the way new experiences stretch us, everything seemed a bit magical.

Still, I wanted to find the queen.

In my mind, the queen was the center of the colony. She was the leader, and laying my eyes on her for the first time seemed a necessary measure of success as a new beekeeper.

I sat down the first frame and removed the second from the hive box. I did my best to look at each of the bees. Then, I gently returned that frame for another. I repeated the process, moving as gently as possible from frame to frame. Occasionally, I'd give a puff of smoke when the girls seemed to get more aggressive.

After going through the upper and lower boxes, and still not finding the queen, I started over. I could see lots of capped brood, a sure sign of the presence of a healthy laying queen. There was honey in other parts of the hive. Everything seemed as I expected based on my limited knowledge.

Starting over, I carefully searched from frame, to frame, to frame.

Finally, I found her. I remember exclaiming out loud, "There you are!"

Even though I was excited to finally meet her, she was indifferent. Her job was to lay eggs, not greet strange men. Aloof, she carried on, seemingly oblivious to my existence.

Purpose

The queen bee is revered because she has a special and distinct purpose. She is the only one with the job of laying eggs. It is common to make the mistake of considering her to be in charge. To imagine her as the leader, or the rest of the colony as her minions, is a common misconception.

Honeybee hierarchy is not quite so simple.

HOPE & HONEYBEES

The queen bee is not an absolute monarch. Even to suggest she is the boss lady or the foreman is an exaggeration and a misunderstanding of her role.

Astonishingly, a honeybee colony does not have a designated leader. They are led by their purpose and design: to function as a single unit. Yes, they are a group made up of many individuals. However, their lives are so intricately woven together, they will die in the absence of one another's support.

This collaborative form of existence is what entomologists refer to as a superorganism.

William Morton Wheeler created The notion of superorganisms over 100 years ago. Wheeler "described social insect colonies as 'superorganisms' because of the degree to which society members seem to act as a unit."[87] This distinction applies to ants, termites, wasps, and honeybees. Leafcutter ants, for example, have "one of the most complex communication systems known in animals, these ants have the most elaborate caste systems, build air-conditioned nests, and 'invented' agriculture long before humans did, by growing a fungus inside their nests for food."[88]

The level of collaborative effort in a superorganism is inspirational. It gives us hope for how things could be if people worked together as one.

Gaia Vince, writing for the BBC argues this exact definition (of a superorganism) is a way to think of humans. Vince writes that humans, "have now become the dominant force shaping our planet," and our interconnectedness makes us a superorganism.[89] Vince goes on to write that humanity has become a "global network of civilisations with a stream of knowledge already being channeled for human protection."[90]

We have a lot of work to do to reach the level of harmony witnessed in the natural world.

For example, one of the most important harmony-creating aspects of a superorganism comes from a clear definition and adherence to roles. The survival and reproductive efforts of the entire colony require the cooperative submission to collective purpose. Everyone has the group's best interest in mind.

We should all be so hopeful as to see global, human effort arise to the level of intentional harmony seen in the world of insects. With solidarity of purpose, honeybees, ants, and the like exist in their prescribed role as selfless units of the whole.

Their unified purpose defines individual roles and helps each generation thrive.

Roles

There are three types of adult bees in a healthy, thriving colony. Each group "typically consists of... workers, drones, and a queen."[91] Their birth and design determine each individual's responsibilities, expectations, and roles.

Worker bees are "the smallest of the bee castes, but are by far the most numerous."[92] The worker bees are female bees. As previously mentioned, the role of worker bees will change over the course of their life.

The workers are aptly named. They, quite literally, perform every task necessary for the colony to thrive, with the exception of reproduction. The *Mid-Atlantic Apiculture Research and Extension Consortium* provides this partial list of the diverse and demanding tasks required of the female bees in a colony:

- "They secrete the wax used in the hive, and form it into honeycombs.
- They forage for all of the nectar and pollen brought into the hive, and transform the nectar into honey.
- They produce royal jelly to feed to the queen and young larvae.
- They also tend to the needs of the larvae and queens.
- They cap the cells of mature larvae for pupation and remove debris and dead bees from the hive.
- Worker bees defend the hive against intruders and maintain optimal conditions by heating, cooling and ventilating the hive."[93]

Female worker bees are "normally incapable of reproduction; they are unable to mate."[94] However, if a colony loses its queen the worker bees "may begin to lay unfertilized eggs, which develop into drones."[95]

If female worker bees do all the actual work, what is the purpose of the male bees?

The male bees are called drones. They are much larger than worker bees and their body size and bulging eyeballs make them easier to identify. "Honeybee drones do not forage or participate in colony maintenance or defense."[96] The drone has one purpose as a part of the honeybee superorganism: "to fertilize a young queen bee."[97]

If that sounds unfair, or like the male bees have it made, we should consider the presumably frustrating life cycle of the drone bee.

Because their only purpose is to spread the genetic material of the colony, drones exhaust themselves in finding a mate. The drone, making up only about 5% to 15% of the typical bee colony, also submits itself to its predetermined purpose.

Like the other bees, the bee's purpose affects its design. The drone bee has no stinger to defend itself. Instead, drones are equipped with "a huge and elaborate endohallus."[98] Otherwise known as "a bee penis."[99]

The drones go into the wild without any protection; being a male bee is not a great gig. Competition is fierce, and "fewer than 5 in 1,000 drones will get the opportunity to mate with a Queen."[100]

If the male drone fails to mate, it returns to the hive to eat, rest, and try again another day.

On the rare chance that a male drone bee is successful in its efforts to mate, the mating process results in death. His reproductive organs break off, remaining with the queen, drastically shortening the drone's life."[101]

Adding insult to injury, unsuccessful male bees that do manage to remain alive when the autumn chill arrives, are forced out of the hive by the worker bees.

Cold and alone, the virgin drones die by exposure.

We might jokingly say the girls get the last laugh for doing all the work. However, the unfruitful death of the drones is simply a part of their purpose. Drone bees have nothing to add when the mating season ends. As the colony hunkers down for the cold winter months, they focus on protecting the queen and keeping her warm.

Finally, we get to the queen. Again, it is somewhat mistaken to think of her as the tyrannical ruler. She is no despot. Unique in her design, the queen is also a slave to purpose: "Her function… is one of production."[102]

In each healthy colony of honeybees, there will be one queen.[103] During winter, after the drones have been expelled, the worker bees will huddle around the queen to keep her warm. Margarita López-Uribe, Ph.D., an Associate Professor of Entomology at Penn State University says bees use various strategies for surviving the cold winter months. "Physiologically and behaviorally, winter honey bees are different from summer bees because they stop rearing brood in the nest and, most importantly, form a thermoregulating cluster."[104] She goes on to explain how they stay warm. "Through the vibration of their flight muscles, honey bees generate heat and maintain the core temperature of the cluster between 77ºF and 95ºF (25ºC and 35ºC)."[105]

When spring arrives, the cluster begins to break as foragers head out in search of resources and other workers start cleaning house. With the change in season, the queen begins to lay eggs. This transformation is triggered when the first pollen is brought home by foraging worker bees.[106]

Once she begins to produce, the work of a queen bee is tireless. Daily, the queen "can lay over 3,000 eggs… that's more than her own body weight in eggs!"[107]

Still, the queen is not in control of the colony. She, too, is driven by purpose. Yes, her role is unique and essential, yet she must produce or be usurped.

The special abilities of the queen allows her to create workers, drones, and (potentially) her own replacement. If the queen fails to produce enough eggs, she will indeed "be replaced (a process called 'supersedure')" by worker bees acting on behalf of the entire colony.[108] The workers will identify a baby bee in larval stage, feed her royal jelly, and groom her to become the next monarch.[109]

Oneness

A honeybee is a simple creature. Understanding the different roles in a colony helps us see how they are also immensely complicated. From the moment it emerges from its larval state, whether it is a queen, worker, or drone, the honeybee goes to work.

Bees are driven by purpose.

United by their cohesive design, they exist in a state of oneness.

The closer you look at these incredible insects, the more you realize they are uniquely adapted to function as a part of a vibrant community. They work together and depend on one another in the ultimate sense.

Their purpose is organically entwined with their existence.

To be a honeybee is to exist dependent on one another. In the truest sense, each individual bee exists for the good of the other bees in their family.

Apart from the mutual support of the community, they will cease to exist.

Like bees, humans clean, care, gather, feed, build, protect, reproduce, and communicate. Unlike the honeybee, we humans often struggle to determine our purpose in life. It is uncommon for someone to state a clear purpose for their existence. It is scarcely the case for a human to say they genuinely exist for the good of others in their community.

Perhaps we could all learn more about opportunities to live as one by studying honeybees.

Directed by their simple purpose, the bees are a model of true unity for all.

11

Unity

In today's divisive world, is it possible to experience unity?

Can we be united with people who believe something different than us?

Can local churches model unity for the world?

The most significant experience of unity I ever had was in the United States Marine Corps. As Marines, we trained, equipped, and organized around a single purpose: Winning.

We had a strong sense of being incredibly powerful. I've often tried to explain how we felt invincible and the enthusiastic optimism we shared. It was not our youth, although we were young. It certainly was not our intelligence; I mean, we were Marines. Not even the strength of our backs could be attributed to what made us feel so strong. Nor was it the massive weapons of destruction we had at our disposal.

What made us feel powerful, truly powerful, was the sense of unity we shared. We knew that no matter what happened, we had one another's back.

We would have died for one another.

We had this strong sense of belonging and an "esprit de corps," or a deep-rooted sense of unity, oneness, and identity as Marines.

Adding to the sense of prowess, we had the support of others outside of our group.

We could call on the Navy if we needed a medic or support from the sea. If we needed additional support from the air, we could call on the Air Force. If we needed help cleaning up the mess we had made, we called on the Army.

Sorry to my Army friends, I couldn't resist.

In all sincerity, if we needed bigger guns and more of them, we could always call on the Army. The Army has the numbers, and although we have fun at one another's expense, the Army brings the fight.

Together, the combined force of the United States Military, backed by the most potent allies on the planet, is a force to reckon with.

However, and this is the point, it was the sense of oneness we had with one another that truly made us feel a part of the most destructive fighting force in the history of the world. Unity creates strength.

Every nation has moments of despairing division and hopeful unity.

We often look back to World War II as an era of great unity in America.

During WWII, people helped out with the war effort however they could. Men and women rallied to the cause. Citizens suffered through mandatory blackouts and food shortages. Families came together and sacrificed for the greater good. Many planted gardens to help ration food.

Everyone was united in their prayers and hope for victory.

In more recent history, most recall the sense of national unity collectively experienced after the September 11 attacks. People remember the stars and stripes on display everywhere. There was an immeasurable surge in patriotism. Internationally, in response to the tragedy, there was almost universal condemnation of terrorism.

It was a fleeting moment of unification.

These historic moments, and others like them, have several common elements of an enemy, cause, and effort.

- **Enemy** - Unifying moments often have an apparent evil to collectively aim our energy and efforts at defeating. The common enemy allows everyone to know the target.
- **Cause** - This agreed-upon enemy gives rise to leaders who rally people to the common cause. They challenge all to rise-up, to stand against, and to be part of the solution.
- **Effort** - Finally, unity comes with collective effort in the face of despair. The majority leans in to do what they can to help out.

The common enemy and unified cause connect people to a joint effort. The result is a common goal and a deep sense of unification. People even identify themselves by their ability to contribute.

One could argue a powerful enemy gives birth to unity.

Today, in the absence of commonality, we seem increasingly divided.

Yet, it is a dangerous exaggeration to say we are more divided than ever. The riots of the 60s, the Civil War, and the Revolutionary War seem far more divisive than our current times. Still, we are increasingly divided, and that division is happening in new, never-imagined ways.

Like the past moments of unity, division is felt by all.

In an effort to increase ratings, news media companies use more and more bombastic terms. Their emotionally charged words wind people up and add to the tension.

Social media gives voices to toxic people. The algorithms, designed to amplify our tendencies toward emotional responses, create viral platforms for unethical people.

Finally, each person's selfish interests boost the division with an inability or unwillingness to serve and sacrifice for one another. Our perceived lack of resources and our desire to have more clout, power, and influence than our neighbors leads us to tear one another down.

We selfishly elevate our wants over the needs of others.

The realization of our divisiveness creates despair.

Applying hope as a solution opens the door to a question. Is it possible for us to experience unity on the local level if there is so much national and global division?

I think, "Yes."

One way to be more united is to recommit ourselves to a sense of unity in Christ.

Rather than following the pattern of negativity in our culture, sincere believers should model an optimistic, hope-filled outlook. Churches should equip people to pursue a lifestyle attractive to those not in a body of faith. Our local gatherings should model unity with love for one another. We, as followers of Christ, should be set apart from the world in our oneness.

The Church, in its purest and original form, still holds the moral high ground. When we embrace a primitive style of Christianity, built on the model recorded for us in the Book of Acts, we set the pace for what is ethical and moral. However, we have to commit to model it with one another. As the world becomes more divisive and secularism grows, the practice of unity in and amongst local churches will become increasingly important.

Each of us, as members of the local church, must commit to model the unity of Jesus Christ.

United

I mentioned earlier the sense of unity I experienced as a young Marine. There is another time I experienced unity in purpose and with great hope. It was at a gathering of local churches.

About ten years ago, I helped lead a mission conference in Dubai, a city in the United Arab Emirates (U.A.E.) famous for its wealth. The U.A.E. is predominantly Muslim. They have laws against sharing the gospel as a Christian.[110]

There is scant freedom of religion. A restrictive set of laws governs churches.

During my trip, I visited the one legally sanctioned Christian church building in Dubai. It was situated far outside of the city. It sat on the outskirts of town. There were no crosses allowed on the outside of the building and so, when they designed it, they made a central hub with four wings. Our host pointed out to us that when you see the building from the air it looks like a giant plus sign. It looks like one of the symbols of the early church. Just look up Greek Crosses and you will see what I mean.

This one cross-shaped building is where all of the legal U.A.E. churches were allowed to gather for worship. It was a humble building uniting all manner of denominations.

Roman Catholics worshiped together in the same building with Eastern Orthodox Churches. Baptists, Charismatics, Independents, Coptics, Anglicans, Seventh Day Adventist, every manner of church denomination met and shared this one building.

Together, they scheduled worship at different times for their congregations.

Together, they shared the upkeep of the building.

Together, they worshiped under one roof in a beautiful show of unity.

The churches united despite their diverse theological perspectives. In their diversity, even though they lived in spiritually hostile territory, they found a sense of oneness.

At one point in the trip, a local pastor asked me about my home church. At the time, I was serving as a local missionary and was supported by Southeast Christian Church in Louisville, Kentucky. Southeast is what you would call a giga-church. It has over 40,000 members and is made up of multiple locations. Many of the satellite campuses are considered mega-churches themselves. They have sites with well over 1,000 attendees.

Southeast is not as well known outside of the Louisville region. It's unlike some of the other more famous churches of similar size. None of the pastors in Dubai had heard of our church.

When my pastor friend in Dubai pressed to understand what denomination I was a part of, I told him, "I'm part of the Christian Churches; it's an independent local church."

He said, "Well, I've never heard of Southeast Christian, but it sounds like you are like us. We are also a 'Christian' church. We are all 'Christian' Churches here. "

The pastor went on to explain how they are not afforded the luxury of division over trivial theological differences. The catholic, protestant, and eastern churches are all one.

They are united in their belief in Jesus Christ.

He asked me if I understood how they can have a sense of unity and yet be divided theologically.

I really didn't know; but, I expected him to say some pithy statement like, "What Would Jesus do, brother?"

What he said was much more powerful. He explained, "I know my Christian brothers and sisters, even though they may practice small things differently than me, or they might interpret scripture in some ways different from me, I know they still believe in Jesus." Then, he added, "I know they will not try to kill me, steal my wife, and sell my children into slavery."

I was immediately humbled. In America, we have the luxury of dividing over minor theological differences. This religious snobbery is a privilege not shared in much of the world.

Another pastor, a Coptic Christian from Egypt who was traveling with us, nodded whole-heartedly to the Emirati pastor's explanation. I understood more fully when my Egyptian friend later shared how his family had suffered under the Muslim Brotherhood. He had suffered terrible things for our shared faith.

Don't miss this point.

The church in Dubai experienced unity because they understood the challenges they were united **against** and, importantly, the God they were **united with**!

This call to unity is threaded throughout the New Testament. In writing to churches facing persecution, Paul often talked about being "united."

The call to oneness makes sense if we look at the context of Paul's culture. If we put ourselves in Paul's first century sandals and walk with him for a bit, we realize the Bible was actually written in an incredibly divisive environment. Although there were not any denominations yet, there were diverse ways of thought. There were various religions and many pagan beliefs.

The Jews hated the pagans, the pagans hated the Jews, the pagans hated other pagans, and everyone agreed on their hate of the newly founded Christian faith.

Because the Christians were new and outnumbered, they were the minority. The people in power had power and the opportunity to attack them.

The Christians, in the first century, were persecuted heavily. Indeed, they were persecuted and often put to death for believing in Jesus Christ.

Despite this friction filled time, Paul writes about being united repetitively. One example can be seen in his letter to the church in Corinth.

In 1 Corinthians 1:10-17, we read this:

> [10] I APPEAL TO YOU, BROTHERS AND SISTERS, IN THE NAME OF OUR LORD JESUS CHRIST, THAT ALL OF YOU AGREE WITH ONE ANOTHER IN WHAT YOU SAY AND THAT THERE BE NO DIVISIONS

> AMONG YOU, BUT THAT YOU BE PERFECTLY UNITED IN MIND AND THOUGHT. ¹¹ MY BROTHERS AND SISTERS, SOME FROM CHLOE'S HOUSEHOLD HAVE INFORMED ME THAT THERE ARE QUARRELS AMONG YOU. ¹² WHAT I MEAN IS THIS: ONE OF YOU SAYS, "I FOLLOW PAUL"; ANOTHER, "I FOLLOW APOLLOS"; ANOTHER, "I FOLLOW CEPHAS"; STILL ANOTHER, "I FOLLOW CHRIST." ¹³ IS CHRIST DIVIDED? WAS PAUL CRUCIFIED FOR YOU? WERE YOU BAPTIZED IN THE NAME OF PAUL? ¹⁴ I THANK GOD THAT I DID NOT BAPTIZE ANY OF YOU EXCEPT CRISPUS AND GAIUS, ¹⁵ SO NO ONE CAN SAY THAT YOU WERE BAPTIZED IN MY NAME. ¹⁶ (YES, I ALSO BAPTIZED THE HOUSEHOLD OF STEPHANAS; BEYOND THAT, I DON'T REMEMBER IF I BAPTIZED ANYONE ELSE.) ¹⁷ FOR CHRIST DID NOT SEND ME TO BAPTIZE, BUT TO PREACH THE GOSPEL—NOT WITH WISDOM AND ELOQUENCE, LEST THE CROSS OF CHRIST BE EMPTIED OF ITS POWER.[111]

Paul urges the church to be united in Christ Jesus alone. Today, Paul's calling for unity challenges us to reject every possible division.

Elsewhere in the New Testament, for example, in the Book of Romans, Paul writes about rejecting our selfish ways, our sinful nature, and pursuing Christ. As he does, the Apostle compels us to unite with Christ and be "set free from sin."

In his call for unity, Paul uses the Greek word, "symphytos." Symphytos means, according to *The Theological Lexicon of the New Testament*: "innate, natural; to be born with, grow with; to be attached or united to or combined with."[112] To further explain, "the verbal adjective *symphytos* means not only 'of the same nature' but also 'growing together.'"[113]

Understanding Paul's Greek gives some insight into what he writes in Romans:6:5-7.

> ⁵ FOR IF WE HAVE BEEN UNITED *[SYMPHYTOS - BORN WITH, ATTACHED OR UNITED OR COMBINED WITH]* WITH *[JESUS CHRIST]* IN A DEATH LIKE HIS, WE WILL CERTAINLY ALSO BE UNITED WITH HIM IN A RESURRECTION LIKE HIS. ⁶ FOR WE KNOW THAT OUR OLD SELF WAS CRUCIFIED WITH HIM SO THAT THE BODY RULED BY SIN MIGHT BE DONE AWAY WITH, THAT WE SHOULD NO LONGER BE SLAVES TO SIN—⁷ BECAUSE ANYONE WHO HAS DIED HAS BEEN SET FREE FROM SIN.[114]

In Paul's example, as he builds up the churches, we see a Christian Spirit of unity and community coming together in Christ. That sense of unity starts with an individual rejection of sin and a communal commitment to Christ.

We, therefore, see universal opportunities for unity born from those united in Christ. And from a call to unity, we can be truly united. United to Christ and one another.

That is why, amid the most terrible persecution, the early Christians could stand with and for one another.

- To share with one another.
- To encourage one another.
- To bear one another's burden.
- To have all things in common with one another.
- To love one another as brothers and sisters, sacrificing for one another in complete love.

This call to unity comes from Paul on repeat.

What about Jesus? Did Christ Himself demonstrate unity?

To answer this question, we need to look no further than those whom Jesus called as His disciples to see how Christ modeled radical unity in love.

In Luke's gospel, Luke 6:13-16, there is a list of the twelve disciples called originally by Jesus.[115]

Amongst this group is Matthew, the Tax Collector, and Simon, called the Zealot.

As a collector of taxes for the Roman authority, Matthew is working for the man. The Romans employ him. He does their dirty work by collecting taxes on his fellow countrymen.

Matthew, the Tax Collector, was called to Jesus and changed.

Simon, the Zealot, was on the opposite side of the spectrum from Matthew, politically speaking. The zealots were a subculture of Jews who wanted to overthrow the Romans and return Israel to an independent state.

Matthew and Simon had very little in common. They were on complete opposite ends of the political spectrum of their time. Yet, here they are, the inner circle of Jesus' ministry.

The sell-out tax collector, alongside the radical, rebellious zealot, were both called to Jesus and transformed.

In Jesus' inner circle, you have a conspirator and enabler, Matthew, walking hand in hand with the radically-minded rebel, Simon. They may be on opposite ends of the political spectrum, yet in Jesus, they are walking together in unity.

A politically divisive duo, brought together at the same table by the One they both called "Lord."

Unity?

Back to our original question: Can we experience unity?

Is it possible?

Yes, it is possible. Only through Jesus Christ can we find unity and become a model of a cohesive body. However, we must come together with Jesus' message as our goal.

His message is love.

If love is insufficient, we must only take stock of the Church's challenges today.

As believers, we do have a common enemy, cause, and effort to unite us.

- We know the **Enemy** is constantly trying to deceive and destroy us, our family, and our children.
- We are given the **Cause** of Christ and His Great Commission to share His message with the world.
- We have a call to the same **Effort**. Leaders like Paul and many others challenge us to see our local community redeemed for the sake of our neighbors and the generations that follow us.

What could unity look like for Churches today?

This communal effort, united in a common cause against a common enemy, might gain traction if we all remember Paul's words to the church in Ephesus.

Ephesians 4:1-6 says this:

> ¹AS A PRISONER FOR THE LORD, THEN, I URGE YOU TO LIVE A LIFE WORTHY OF THE CALLING YOU HAVE RECEIVED. ² BE COMPLETELY HUMBLE AND GENTLE; BE PATIENT, BEARING WITH ONE ANOTHER IN LOVE. ³ MAKE EVERY EFFORT TO KEEP THE UNITY OF THE SPIRIT THROUGH THE BOND OF PEACE. ⁴ THERE IS ONE BODY AND ONE SPIRIT, JUST AS YOU WERE CALLED TO ONE HOPE WHEN YOU WERE CALLED; ⁵ ONE LORD, ONE FAITH, ONE BAPTISM; ⁶ ONE GOD AND FATHER OF ALL, WHO IS OVER ALL AND THROUGH ALL AND IN ALL.[116]

Unity came to the early church the same way it will for us.

It is not from the world, not from the news.

It is not from social media.

Instead, unity comes from a deep commitment to Jesus Christ and His perfect Way.

We don't have to agree in practice or even theology. It is okay for there to be diversity in belief. When we focus on what makes us different from one another, we only amplify our fleshly desire to be more divisive.

Besides, over 2,000 years of church history have proven there is plenty of room for diversity of worship and practice. Importantly, we must continue to seek oneness and unity in the name above all names, in Jesus Christ.

We can step into the goodness of a unified purpose through Him alone. Then, together with one another, we will experience a harvest worthy of His loving sacrifice.

12

Honey

As the flowers bloom in the spring, the honeybee gets to work. Each colony sends out some hopeful scouts. The task of these early emerging bees is simple: find food.

Their work never ends.

The hardworking forager bees fly from flower to flower, collecting nectar. This sugary secretion from plants will become the golden substance of divine sweetness we call honey!

Honey-making is a complicated and time-consuming process.

The raw material of honey is nectar from flowering plants. Ingested by bees, it is "broken down into simple sugars."[117] Then, as the foraging bees return to the hive, they "pass their nectar loads by trophallaxis" (the direct process of food or liquids moved from one individual to another).[118] [119]

If you have ever heard people jokingly call honey bee-barf, now you know why.

The process of handing off the fluid to receiver bees with "repeated regurgitation and re-ingestion of nectar droplets, also known as 'tongue lashing behaviour,' ... occurs for extended periods."[120] Eventually, the honey is "stored inside the honeycomb." [121] The bees work together to fan the honeycomb with their wings. This "constant fanning of the bees' wings causes evaporation."[122] Nectar has to be "concentrated to more than 80% for storage in the nest."[123]

Once the honey is ripened or dehydrated properly, it is sealed with a layer of wax.

The color and flavor of honey varies. The source of "the nectar collected by the bees" affects the finished product.[124] "For example, honey made from orange blossom nectar might be light in color, whereas honey from avocado or wildflowers might have a dark amber color."[125] The nectar source will also create subtle to profound differences in the taste.

Each hive will produce as much as "55 pounds of surplus honey each year."[126] Beekeepers, being cautious not to take too much of the bees' stored food, will then harvest the surplus "by collecting the honeycomb frames and scraping off the wax cap."[127] With the caps removed, they "are placed in an extractor" and spun at a fast rate.[128] The centrifugal forces of the spinning motion draw the honey from the comb. It is then filtered and stored in clean containers for distribution.[129]

Honey production and harvesting are time-consuming and sticky tasks. However, for most beekeepers, harvesting honey is the sweet-tasting goal of all their efforts.

Producing honey is a massive undertaking for the beekeeper. Like any endeavor, there is a risk of loss and no small amount of danger.

Honey production is not always profitable.

Small hobbyists and large apiarists will often sell their surplus supply in markets. A single hive can earn as much as $500 a year if the bees successfully produce an adequate surplus. However, a British beekeeper named David Evans chronicled the success of his four-hive operation in a recent blog post at *TheApiarist.org*.

Evans factored in expenses related to miticides and equipment. He did not factor in the time involved. All of his work produced a meager profit. His conclusion was, "No one is going to get rich quickly on £100 ($130 USD) per hive per year."[130] Admittedly, he did not factor in the joy and other intangible benefits of beekeeping (i.e., crop pollination and production of alternative resources such as bee balm or candles).

If beekeeping to harvest honey is a lot of work, we should remember it is incredibly challenging for the bees. "A single honey bee forager will only collect" a small amount of nectar, "about the size of two drops of water, per trip."[131] "By the end of summer, a large colony will have stored over 100 lbs, or 45 kgs, of honey."[132] Each bee will visit "about two million flowers and fly 50,000 miles (80,000 km) to make one pound (454 g) of honey."[133] Therefore, "a single honey bee makes about one-twelfth of a teaspoon of honey during its lifetime."[134]

Honey bottles come in many shapes and sizes. In the U.S., it is common to find bottles of honey sold by the pound. Bees will travel a distance equal to two full trips around the earth to produce a single pound of honey.[135] It will take about "12 honeybees 72 weeks (six weeks each) to make a single teaspoon of honey."[136] There are 64 teaspoons in a pound of honey. Therefore, "that's 768 honeybees working 4,608 weeks (six weeks each) to make a pound of honey."[137]

Importantly, it is not just about the honey.

As they work, bees and other pollinator insects also pollinate our crops. Writing for the *Defenders of Wildlife,* Taft reports on "The economic ramifications" of losing these hard-working pollinators. Honeybees, together with other wild bees, "pollinate 70 crop species out of 100 that feed around 90% of the world's population."[138]

The next time you put a bottle of local honey in your shopping cart, consider the tremendous amount of work that has gone into it. Each bottle of honey represents an amazing effort from our bees.

It is not only about the honey; their work puts food on the table. The efforts of honey-making insects undergird our entire food chain.

Senses

Understanding the global impact and hard work that goes into honey production makes it all the more sweet as a treat. It is arguably the most delicious natural substance on the planet. The golden color, enticing aroma, and delicious taste seduce us to have just a bit more.

Honey awakens our senses in a uniquely organic way. Yet, is there a better way to explain this complex sugar than simply saying, "It is sweet."

In the basement of my local church, Tunnel Hill Christian Church, a group of local beekeepers meets monthly. The Spring Valley Beekeepers group consists of 50 to 60 (mostly hobbyist) local keepers who gather to share best practices. We share expertise, frustrations, and opportunities. Common topics of discussion range from the price of sugar to good deals on equipment. It is a great time to encourage one another and ask, "How are your bees doing?"

John Schellenberger, our local club's leader and the President of the Indiana Beekeeping Association, has organized a honey-tasting contest for the past couple of years. It always draws a crowd, and John intentionally gets local politicians and public servants to participate in the process.

In John's words, "It is good to educate people outside of our club on the importance of what bees do for our world." I agree with his efforts and can think of no better way to build excitement than to have them taste samples of honey from the dozens of entries.

The experience encourages local leaders to consider our pollinators' vital agricultural role.

The honey-tasting contest works by having beekeepers submit a jar of their honey for submission. The jars are blackish. The dark color negates any bias one might have over honey's different colors or shades. The jars all look the same except for a tracking number. This effort removes the opportunity for labels, bottling designs, or relationships to distract the judges.

The best-tasting honey wins.

One year, I opted out of the competition to experience what it was like to be a judge. It wasn't a hard decision to make. Who wouldn't want to sample 30 different bottles of local honey!? The judges said, "So long seasonal allergies," considering the benefits of tasting so much honey.

Together with the other judges, we gathered around trays with several honey jars and used tasting spoons. We dipped them in each bottle, allowing the honey to fill our senses and strike our palate. We'd toss the dirty spoon away, cleanse our palate, grab a clean spoon, and repeat the tasting.

Each of us carried a clipboard. We individually took notes of each sample that impressed us.

The honey we were sampling came from all across Floyd County, Indiana, and the surrounding counties. The diversity in flavors, even for such a small region, was terrific.

Some of the flavors we experienced were:

- Caramel
- Orange
- Strawberry
- Almond
- Floral
- Maple
- Earthy
- Blackberry
- Nutty
- Oaky
- Spicy

One jar stood out to me. It had a sweet, smokey oakness to it. We jokingly laughed that those bees must have gotten into someone's bourbon.

At some point, you would think you'd tire of different honeys. You would be wrong.

Each sample brought a new sensation. More than one bottle elicited an audible gasp as one of the judges experienced an unexpected, delightful sensation.

I must admit I sampled from the bottle I chose as my favorite about nine times. I almost felt bad about all the taster spoons I was wasting, but it was so amazing! I couldn't resist!

Honey is more than a golden liquid served as a natural sweetener. It represents the diversity of local hobbyists and farmers alike. Each taste is a testimony of God's unique ability to design the natural world to delight us.

Although honey harvesting may be a lot of work, anyone can tell you it is well worth the effort.

13

Harvest

One of the hidden blessings of working outdoors is the organic way the garden brings God's truth alive.

Jesus' teachings, for example, on the plentiful harvest in Matthew 9, come to life. Beginning in verse 35, we read about the challenge of finding workers to go into the harvest fields.

> 35 AND JESUS WENT THROUGHOUT ALL THE CITIES AND VIL-LAGES, TEACHING IN THEIR SYNAGOGUES AND PROCLAIMING THE GOSPEL OF THE KINGDOM AND HEALING EVERY DISEASE AND EVERY AFFLICTION. 36 WHEN HE SAW THE CROWDS, HE HAD COMPASSION FOR THEM, BECAUSE THEY WERE HARASSED AND HELPLESS, LIKE SHEEP WITHOUT A SHEPHERD. 37 THEN HE SAID TO HIS DISCIPLES, "THE HARVEST IS PLENTIFUL, BUT THE LABORERS ARE FEW; 38 THEREFORE PRAY EARNESTLY TO THE LORD OF THE HARVEST TO SEND OUT LABORERS INTO HIS HARVEST."[139]

Thinking of the local church in agricultural terms helps passages like this spring to life. Jesus tells us, "The harvest is plentiful… and to pray, "to the Lord of the harvest to send out," people to work the harvest.

In the past, I have read this passage and thought of it as a calling for people to go out and do the church's work. When I led in children's and family ministry, I used it as a rallying point to get people to volunteer. It is, after all, a call to action and a challenge to serve.

However, I think we can look at this passage a little more intently with agrarian lenses. In fact, we see at least three gardens throughout the Bible. This trio of gardens allows us to frame this question: If Jesus is telling us, "the work is plentiful but the laborers are few," then... what is our role in the work of the Church?

How can we each help in the harvest?

The First Garden

The world begins in Genesis 1. In Genesis 2, humankind's relationship with God begins! It all begins in the Garden of Eden.

The Genesis account explains to us how the first Garden was created by God and entrusted to humanity.

Genesis 2:7–9 records for us the nature of this relationship.

> [7] ...THEN THE LORD GOD FORMED THE MAN OF DUST FROM THE GROUND AND BREATHED INTO HIS NOSTRILS THE BREATH OF LIFE, AND THE MAN BECAME A LIVING CREATURE. [8] AND THE LORD GOD PLANTED A GARDEN IN EDEN, IN THE EAST, AND THERE HE PUT THE MAN WHOM HE HAD FORMED. [9] AND OUT OF THE GROUND THE LORD GOD MADE TO SPRING UP EVERY TREE THAT IS PLEASANT TO THE SIGHT AND GOOD FOR FOOD.

> THE TREE OF LIFE WAS IN THE MIDST OF THE GARDEN,
> AND THE TREE OF THE KNOWLEDGE OF GOOD AND EVIL.[140]

The imagery here is so fantastic.

You can imagine God forming life in His image from the earth. He is the potter; we are the clay.

If you have ever gardened, you know the delight of plunging your hands into rich, fertile soil. Weeks later, you experience the joy of seedlings springing up from your work.

For God, I imagine His garden, new and teeming with life, was similar. God must have felt a deep satisfaction and joy filled hope. The Genesis account reveals to us part of what He experienced. His instantaneous delight in His new Creation is recorded for us in Genesis 1:31.

> [31] GOD SAW ALL THAT HE HAD MADE, AND IT WAS VERY GOOD."[141]

Eden is the first garden. There, in a heavenly setting, God plants humanity.

The intended harvest of Eden is an eternal relationship of hope with the Creator. The hopeful yield from the original garden stems from our Designer. He created us for hope, love, and community.

The Garden of Eden began in perfect order.

However, the Genesis story also tells how sin enters the garden. Sin breaks the community designed by God. The lawlessness of man unleashed into paradise leads to the final garden. A garden we read about in Revelation.

The Final Garden

The ultimate garden is stewarded and worked by humanity. It is reaped, or harvested, by Christ.

In Revelation, the Church and all souls find themselves measured.

In chapter 14 of John's prophetic vision, the Book of Revelation, we read about "The Harvest of the Earth."

> [14] THEN I LOOKED, AND BEHOLD, A WHITE CLOUD, AND SEATED ON THE CLOUD ONE LIKE A SON OF MAN, WITH A GOLDEN CROWN ON HIS HEAD, AND A SHARP SICKLE IN HIS HAND. [15] AND ANOTHER ANGEL CAME OUT OF THE TEMPLE, CALLING WITH A LOUD VOICE TO HIM WHO SAT ON THE CLOUD, "PUT IN YOUR SICKLE, AND REAP, FOR THE HOUR TO REAP HAS COME, FOR THE HARVEST OF THE EARTH IS FULLY RIPE." [16] SO HE WHO SAT ON THE CLOUD SWUNG HIS SICKLE ACROSS THE EARTH, AND THE EARTH WAS REAPED.[142]

In this final garden, we see the fruit of the earth is ripe.

Autumn has come, and Jesus returns to swing, "his sickle across the earth." A, "sickle," of course, being an ancient tool used to harvest wheat and other grains. Imagine a manually operated weed-eater with the same job as a combine-tractor. A sickle is the menacing weapon often portrayed in the hand of the Grim Reaper.

In this last garden, we glimpse the end of times and Earth's final days. Here, as Christ returns as the conquering King, all is measured.

The final garden will account for all that was unleashed, good and bad, from the time of the first garden.

You and I exist in a time between the first and final gardens.

The Present Garden

The Bible gives us an account of the first garden in Genesis and the final one is foretold in Revelation. How then do we get from A to B, from Alpha to Omega, from beginning to end?

Well, this is what makes Jesus' teachings so poignant and enduring.

We are the present garden.

The present garden is the one Jesus is referring to in Matt 9:37.

> [37] THEN HE SAID TO HIS DISCIPLES, "THE HARVEST IS PLENTIFUL, BUT THE LABORERS ARE FEW; [38] THEREFORE PRAY EARNESTLY TO THE LORD OF THE HARVEST TO SEND OUT LABORERS INTO HIS HARVEST."[143]

The Apostle Luke also recorded these words from Jesus. Luke writes about this teaching just after Jesus has explained the cost of following Him. Jesus warns about the despairing challenges we face in this sin-broken world.

The despair adds to a sense of urgency. It amplifies the call to action.

In the present garden, we have been prepared and sent by Jesus to be a part of the harvest. Importantly, we are laborers bringing home the work He has done.

Luke records Jesus' teaching in this manner, this is Luke 10:1-3.

> [1] AFTER THIS THE LORD APPOINTED SEVENTY-TWO OTHERS AND SENT THEM ON AHEAD OF HIM, TWO BY TWO, INTO EVERY TOWN AND PLACE WHERE HE HIMSELF WAS ABOUT TO GO. [2] AND HE SAID TO THEM, "THE HARVEST IS PLENTIFUL, BUT THE LABORERS ARE FEW. THEREFORE PRAY EARNESTLY TO THE LORD OF THE HARVEST TO SEND OUT LABORERS INTO HIS HARVEST. [3] GO YOUR WAY; BEHOLD, I AM SENDING YOU OUT AS LAMBS IN THE MIDST OF WOLVES.[144]

We the people of the local church are to do the work of the Church.

We are to labor...

- Despite the dangers.
- Regardless of the costs.
- In the face of many hopeless challenges.

Wolves be damned.

We are to continue to hope because He is faithful.

Jesus prepares us. He goes ahead of us. He tills, plants, weeds and waters the ground. The people of the Church harvest the work He has done.

MICHAEL J. CHANLEY

Ripe for the Picking

Brad Tate, a church planter in Howell, Michigan and the founding pastor of Agape City Church, helped me to see this teaching from Jesus in a new light.

Living in a state renowned for apple orchards helped Brad to see the sense of urgency connected to harvesting time. When the apples are ripe, there is a narrow window of opportunity. A limited amount of time exists before the apples go bad.

My friend Brad's point, "If we are not careful; we miss the moment."

The end result is wasted opportunity. A failed harvest.

Of course, there is only so much one person can do on their own. A closer examination of Matthew's text, if we go through it word by word, provides a deeper spiritual truth. It reveals more of Jesus' intent in His teaching and about our present hope.

Verse 35 reveals Jesus' threefold ministry of teaching, preaching, and healing.[145]

> [35] AND JESUS WENT THROUGHOUT ALL THE CITIES AND VILLAGES, TEACHING IN THEIR SYNAGOGUES AND PROCLAIMING THE GOSPEL OF THE KINGDOM AND HEALING EVERY DISEASE AND EVERY AFFLICTION.[146]

Then, we read that Jesus sees the people in their present state as he does this. They are harassed, helpless, and lost ("like sheep without a shepherd"[147]).

> ³⁶ WHEN HE SAW THE CROWDS, HE HAD COMPASSION FOR THEM, BECAUSE THEY WERE HARASSED AND HELPLESS, LIKE SHEEP WITHOUT A SHEPHERD.¹⁴⁸

Does this not sound like the despairing world we live in?

We see people without hope everywhere. They are harassed and helpless. Most of us have felt lost and a bit like sheep needing a guide at some point in our lives.

Finally, Jesus presents an urgent solution to harvest the crop before it is lost. His solution is to send out His disciples. We, as His followers, are the answer.

> ³⁷ THEN HE SAID TO HIS DISCIPLES, "THE HARVEST IS PLENTIFUL, BUT THE LABORERS ARE FEW; ³⁸ THEREFORE PRAY EARNESTLY TO THE LORD OF THE HARVEST TO SEND OUT LABORERS INTO HIS HARVEST."¹⁴⁹

We may look at this calling and say, "I can't teach."

We might argue, "I can't preach."

Indeed, most of us could attest, "I'm no doctor; I can't heal the sick."

When we limit ourselves in this manner, we miss the point. As willing laborers, we are not to focus on our weaknesses. We find hope in His strength, and it becomes our strength.

In John 4:35-38, Jesus is teaching and using another agricultural analogy. He tells the disciples to read the room.

> ³¹ MEANWHILE THE DISCIPLES WERE URGING HIM, SAYING, "RABBI, EAT." ³² BUT HE SAID TO THEM, "I HAVE FOOD TO EAT THAT YOU DO NOT KNOW ABOUT." ³³ SO THE DISCIPLES SAID TO ONE ANOTHER, "HAS ANYONE BROUGHT HIM SOMETHING TO EAT?" ³⁴ JESUS SAID TO THEM, "MY FOOD IS TO DO THE WILL OF HIM WHO SENT ME AND TO ACCOMPLISH HIS WORK. ³⁵ DO YOU NOT SAY, 'THERE ARE YET FOUR MONTHS, THEN COMES THE HARVEST'? LOOK, I TELL YOU, LIFT UP YOUR EYES, AND SEE THAT THE FIELDS ARE WHITE FOR HARVEST. ³⁶ ALREADY THE ONE WHO REAPS IS RECEIVING WAGES AND GATHERING FRUIT FOR ETERNAL LIFE, SO THAT SOWER AND REAPER MAY REJOICE TOGETHER. ³⁷ FOR HERE THE SAYING HOLDS TRUE, 'ONE SOWS AND ANOTHER REAPS.' ³⁸ I SENT YOU TO REAP THAT FOR WHICH YOU DID NOT LABOR. OTHERS HAVE LABORED, AND YOU HAVE ENTERED INTO THEIR LABOR."[150]

According to Jesus, the more urgent work is a willingness to go into the ever-present garden mentioned in Luke and Matthew. John reminds us to be ready and willing.

Yes, we do have to work. When we do, we might reap a harvest from our labors. According to Jesus, when we are willing to follow Him, we will also reap what we have not sown.[151]

We reap the hope of His harvest.

We have entered the labor of those hope-filled generations who came before us.

I remember helping my mom in the garden when I was a child. It would take me about three minutes to get distracted and to start throwing dirt clods in the air to try and get the cats to chase them.

However, my mom would keep working. Planting, pulling weeds, watering the garden, staking the tomatoes. She would spend time in the garden each week, often daily.

Then, whenever things ripened up, I'd get excited about helping a little more. I mean, who doesn't get excited about reaching up and plucking a ripe tomato or strawberry off of the vine and eating it right there!?

Much like the present garden Jesus has prepared for us, I was entering the blessing of someone else's work.

Our Hope

I think Jesus makes it clear that the hard work has already been done here in the present garden. He has gone ahead of us and prepared everything. The most challenging jobs are complete. We just have to open our eyes and receive the blessing. We must be willing to go out and participate in the harvest.

Perhaps at the deepest roots of Jesus' garden analogy are the seeds of hope.

We do not have to look at the world as a cursed place full of thorns. Instead, Christ tells us, as the master gardener, that He has prepared a harvest ahead of us. As John writes, we simply need to "enter into their labor" and join in the hope of harvest.

One practical and simple action step we can take is to practice the discipline of prayer with more intentionality. Matthew 9:38 says: "[38] therefore pray earnestly to the Lord of the harvest to send out laborers into his harvest."[152]

Using this verse as a focus, you could set a recurring reminder on your phone to pray each day at 9:38. Then, when your alarm goes off, take time to ask God to help you be part of the solution. Join Him in the harvest and, "pray earnestly," for the Master Gardener to lead the way.

Another opportunity to aid the laborers' efforts is to redouble your efforts to talk to people about your faith. On a weekly or daily basis, we can each ask ourselves:

- Who can I talk to about God's love?
- How can I model forgiveness and mercy in my family?
- Who in my present local garden needs to hear about the hope I've found in Jesus?

Together, we can make a difference.

You and I are somewhere between the beginning of the Church in Genesis and the harvesting of the Church in Revelation. Here in the present, we have a clear calling to be one of the laborers helping Jesus bring in the harvest.

There is plenty of work for each of us to do. We just need to be willing to go. When we do, those simple things which have already been prepared before us, are fulfilled.

We join the harvest and serve as a part of the Church.

We serve as harvesters and sowers of hope.

We go so all may know the joy of His perfect hope-giving love.

14

Love

At the end of John's gospel, the disciples have lost hope.

In their despair, as they reel and struggle with the jarring fact of Jesus' death, burial, and resurrection, they fall back into the familiar habits of their past lives. We can only imagine the emotional turmoil they experienced as they realized their leader was not setting up a worldly kingdom.

Their broken expectations and crushed dreams must have left them with much to process.

Like people lost without purpose, the disciples return to what they know best. They go fishing.

Adding to their frustrations, we read that even this produces no profit. Their nets are empty.

The confused actions of the disciples are a poignant reminder of how far they have come in following Jesus. The despair of the old way, the path before Jesus came into their lives, must have resurfaced. Empty nets became overwhelming reminders of the hopelessness in their hearts.

Yet, into this darkness, Jesus reenters the story. He uses this moment to remind His followers that He has called them to be completely changed and transformed. He has challenged them to become fishers of men.

The writer of John explains how Jesus comes to the shore and calls out to His disciples. At first, they do not recognize Him.

> ⁵ HE CALLED OUT TO THEM,
> "FRIENDS, HAVEN'T YOU ANY FISH?"
> "NO," THEY ANSWERED.
> ⁶ HE SAID, "THROW YOUR NET ON THE RIGHT SIDE OF THE BOAT AND YOU WILL FIND SOME." WHEN THEY DID, THEY WERE UNABLE TO HAUL THE NET IN BECAUSE OF THE LARGE NUMBER OF FISH.[153]

Jesus gives them a simple instruction; they choose to obey. As they do, their fishing nets are miraculously filled and overflowing.

John, the gospel writer, then recognizes Jesus. As he proclaims, "It is the Lord!"[154] Peter moves to action; he immediately jumps in and begins swimming to the shore. The others follow, bringing the boats and towing the haul of fish with them.

Together again on the beach, they have breakfast with Jesus. At the end of an evening of despair, Jesus restores their purpose and reminds them of their calling.

He gives meaning to life.

He restores hope.

To do so, Jesus leverages His trademark: unconditional, self-sacrificing love.

The Rock

Recorded next in John's account is a love-filled dialogue.

It births hope.

We must dig into Peter's backstory to understand this incredible conversation in the second half of John 21 and its application to our lives.

We meet Peter at the beginning of John's gospel. The last few verses of chapter one record the calling of Jesus' disciples as Christ embarks on His earthly mission.

John 1:40-42 introduces us to Simon, also known as Simon Peter. The same Peter who is fishing at the end of John's book.

> 40 ANDREW, SIMON PETER'S BROTHER, WAS ONE OF THE TWO WHO HEARD WHAT JOHN HAD SAID AND WHO HAD FOLLOWED JESUS. 41 THE FIRST THING ANDREW DID WAS TO FIND HIS BROTHER SIMON [THAT'S PETER] AND TELL HIM, "WE HAVE FOUND THE MESSIAH" (THAT IS, THE CHRIST). 42 AND HE BROUGHT HIM TO JESUS. JESUS LOOKED AT HIM AND SAID, "YOU ARE SIMON SON OF JOHN. YOU WILL BE CALLED CEPHAS" (WHICH, WHEN TRANSLATED, IS PETER).[155]

Jesus foretells Simon's name being changed to Peter. In doing so, Christ also predicts this man's importance in founding His church.

Next, Jesus beckons His new disciples to a simple calling:

43 ... "FOLLOW ME."[156]

John briefly mentions Peter's name change at the beginning of their relationship. He chooses to focus His account on Jesus. However, the other gospel writers go into much more detail about this transformation.

Matthew is added to the group later in Jesus' ministry. In Matthew's account, we see the moment Jesus publicly calls Simon, "Peter." Again, we know it is not the first time Jesus has called Peter by a new name because John recorded the first time it happened.

However, essential to understanding the significance of this transformation, Matthew gives us details of the "why" behind the name change.

Matthew 16:13-20 records the moment.

> [13] WHEN JESUS CAME TO THE REGION OF CAESAREA PHILIPPI, HE ASKED HIS DISCIPLES, "WHO DO PEOPLE SAY THE SON OF MAN IS?" [14] THEY REPLIED, "SOME SAY JOHN THE BAPTIST; OTHERS SAY ELIJAH; AND STILL OTHERS, JEREMIAH OR ONE OF THE PROPHETS." [15] "BUT WHAT ABOUT YOU?" HE ASKED. "WHO DO YOU SAY I AM?" [16] SIMON PETER ANSWERED, "YOU ARE THE MESSIAH, THE SON OF THE LIVING GOD." [17] JESUS REPLIED, "BLESSED ARE YOU, SIMON SON OF JONAH, FOR THIS WAS NOT REVEALED TO YOU BY FLESH AND BLOOD, BUT BY MY FATHER IN HEAVEN. [18] AND I TELL YOU THAT YOU ARE PETER, [E] AND ON THIS ROCK I WILL BUILD MY CHURCH, AND THE GATES OF HADES WILL NOT OVERCOME IT. [19] I WILL GIVE YOU THE KEYS OF THE KINGDOM OF HEAVEN; WHATEVER YOU BIND ON EARTH WILL BE

> BOUND IN HEAVEN, AND WHATEVER YOU LOOSE ON EARTH WILL BE LOOSED IN HEAVEN." 20 THEN HE ORDERED HIS DISCIPLES NOT TO TELL ANYONE THAT HE WAS THE MESSIAH.[157]

Jesus proclaims Peter is of particular significance because his confession of Jesus as "...the Messiah, the Son of the living God." is foundational. At the same time, Jesus knows Peter will help build His Church.

Simon becomes known as Peter.

His name becomes a constant reminder of Jesus' prediction of the crucial, ground-laying work of the Church Peter will do in the future.

This foretelling of Peter's influence is not Jesus's only prediction about Peter. Later in John's gospel, Jesus also predicts Peter's denial.

Jesus later tells His disciples he will be going away.

> 33 "MY CHILDREN, I WILL BE WITH YOU ONLY A LITTLE LONGER. YOU WILL LOOK FOR ME, AND JUST AS I TOLD THE JEWS, SO I TELL YOU NOW: WHERE I AM GOING, YOU CANNOT COME.[158]

Then, He gives them (and us) a new command. We read it in John 13:34-38.

> 34 "A NEW COMMAND I GIVE YOU: LOVE ONE ANOTHER. AS I HAVE LOVED YOU, SO YOU MUST LOVE ONE ANOTHER. 35 BY THIS EVERYONE WILL KNOW THAT YOU ARE MY DISCIPLES, IF YOU LOVE ONE ANOTHER."[159]

Upon hearing this, Peter gets stuck in the moment. He seems hooked on the fact Jesus is leaving. In this critical moment, Peter doesn't ask, "How, Lord, how do we love one another?"

No.

By contrast, Peter focuses only on Jesus' plans to leave. Peter despairs.

> [36] SIMON PETER ASKED HIM, "LORD, WHERE ARE YOU GOING?" JESUS REPLIED, "WHERE I AM GOING, YOU CANNOT FOLLOW NOW, BUT YOU WILL FOLLOW LATER." [37] PETER ASKED, "LORD, WHY CAN'T I FOLLOW YOU NOW? I WILL LAY DOWN MY LIFE FOR YOU."[160]

Peter boldly proclaims complete allegiance to Jesus. He claims to be willing to go the distance, face death, and give up his life to defend His Lord.

Jesus knows better. He knows the real Peter.

> [38] THEN JESUS ANSWERED, "WILL YOU REALLY LAY DOWN YOUR LIFE FOR ME? VERY TRULY I TELL YOU, BEFORE THE ROOSTER CROWS, YOU WILL DISOWN ME THREE TIMES!"[161]

Later in John, we read the fulfillment of Peter's predicted betrayal of Jesus. As it turns out, Peter, the one to whom Jesus said in Matthew's account: "... on this rock I will build my church, and the gates of Hades will not overcome it..." falls as Jesus had foretold.[162]

In John 18, Peter's true character is revealed. The proud man unwittingly fulfills the prophecy of Jesus.

Peter stumbles.

He betrays Jesus—the rock breaks.

Peter acts just as Jesus said he would.

What a powerful story Peter has!? Here is a simple man called to serve the most extraordinary person ever to walk the Earth. The simple fisherman is lifted high as an example. Yet, Peter is also predicted to fail.

Like Icarus, Peter rises to the peak of success but stumbles. He crashes and burns.

Agape

Peter's backstory frames a more complete understanding of the final dialogue in John's gospel. We are not simply reading about a conversation between Jesus and His disciples; instead, it is an insightful example of God's complete love. Jesus pours out absolute forgiveness and restoration. He applies grace and mercy, even to a traitor like Peter, who has failed Christ in His time of great need.

John 21:15 begins the final interaction between Peter and Jesus. They are having breakfast on the lake shore. The disciples have just landed their boat and stepped into a moment with Christ. Peter is still soaking wet from hastily swimming to greet Jesus.

Together, they dine on the fish Jesus has prepared for them.

> [15] **WHEN THEY HAD FINISHED EATING, JESUS SAID TO SIMON PETER, "SIMON SON OF JOHN, DO YOU LOVE ME MORE THAN THESE?"**[163]

First, let's not miss the fact Jesus is referring to Peter by his original name. He calls him "Simon, son of John." The reference to his given name surely reminded Peter of who he was before Jesus. No doubt, it reminded everyone of where he began and how he had failed. Jesus gets back to the very root of the man, even reconnecting Peter's name to his earthly father.

It's as if Jesus looks into the heart of the fallen apostle and says, "I see you for who you are."

A closer look at John 21:15 reveals Jesus' use of the Greek verb "agape." Agape means love, but it is love in the utmost and sacrificial sense.[164] It is not physical, intimate love, nor fleeting, gushy feelings. Agape implies absolute and self-sacrificing love. It is the exact type of love demonstrated repeatedly by Jesus.

A contrasting example of agape love comes from earlier in John's gospel. In John 12:43, agape is used to explain how the Jewish leaders had rejected Jesus. John 12:43 says: "[43]... for they loved human praise more than praise from God."[165] The English word translated as "love" in this passage also comes from "agape." It has the effect of saying the leaders had absolute love for the praise of the people. People pleasing was more important to them than pleasing God. They had put their hope in man, instead of in God.

Alternatively, Jesus, in His "new command" to the disciples, uses agape to explain how we, His disciples, should love one another. Jesus, in John 13:34-35, says:

> ³⁴ "A NEW COMMAND I GIVE YOU: LOVE ONE ANOTHER. AS I HAVE LOVED YOU, SO YOU MUST LOVE ONE ANOTHER. ³⁵ BY THIS EVERYONE WILL KNOW THAT YOU ARE MY DISCIPLES, IF YOU LOVE ONE ANOTHER."[166]

Each English use of love in this passage is the Greek word "agape." Jesus is talking about self-sacrificing love. The complete, dies-to-itself love modeled on the cross. Jesus commands us to the highest type of love possible.

Jesus commands us to follow His example of agape love for one another.

Understanding the meaning of "agape" love highlights the despair in Peter's response to Jesus. The Lord's appeal to restore Peter at breakfast leads the broken-down man to further introspection.

Phileo

How does Peter respond to this appeal for Jesus' complete love in John 21?

Let's look at Peter's response.

> ... "YES, LORD," [PETER] SAID, "YOU KNOW THAT I LOVE YOU."[167]

When Peter replies, he says, "... you know... " and uses the Greek verb, "oida."[168] This verb implies he is saying to Jesus, "You have seen through my past actions; it has been made evident to you."

To paraphrase Peter's words to Jesus, he says, "It's obvious because you witnessed the limits of my love."

We can be critical of Peter's response. The man does not reply with the same "agape" love Christ has asked of him. Instead, the soaking wet fisherman replies using the Greek word, "phileo."[169] In doing so, Peter confesses a type of brotherly love or a deep, friendly affection.

The disciple does not reciprocate the same self-sacrifice in his love.

Therefore, by his choice of words, the fallen disciple says to Jesus, "You have just witnessed my betrayal, and obviously, you know from my past actions I do not sacrificially love you."

To further paraphrase Peter, he is saying, "You know I don't love you the way you love me."

Peter friend zones Jesus.

Jesus could have responded with condemnation and judgment. Instead, grace permeates His response.

> "JESUS SAID, "FEED MY LAMBS."[170]

Jesus commands Peter to do the bare minimum for the simplest and most innocent of His followers.

Then, Jesus continues in John 21:16.

> [16] AGAIN JESUS SAID, "SIMON SON OF JOHN, DO YOU LOVE ME?"

Jesus again uses "agape." He uses sacrificial, complete love in His inquiry.

Peter also repeats himself.

> ... HE [PETER] ANSWERED, "YES, LORD, YOU KNOW THAT I LOVE YOU." ["PHILEO" LOVE]

Peter stays in the friend zone, perhaps in despair. He says again, "You have witnessed my love for you, that it is not self-sacrificing, but I do love you like a dear brother."

Jesus persists with grace and open arms.

> ... JESUS SAID, "TAKE CARE OF MY SHEEP."

By "take care," Jesus implies Peter is to be a shepherd. He commands him to tend, lead, or guide the followers of Jesus.

It's worth noting Jesus also changes from a charge to feed little baby lambs to include the entire flock of sheep. His repeated command, with subtle changes, implies Peter is to be a leader in the church family.

Jesus is not finished.

> [17]THE THIRD TIME HE SAID TO HIM, "SIMON SON OF JOHN, DO YOU LOVE ME?"

In this third question, Jesus changes from "agape" love to the "phileo" love Peter has used in his responses.

Jesus meets Peter where he is.

Jesus asks, do you, "phileo," love me? As He does, Jesus speaks into the heart of the downtrodden Peter. He asks, "Do you truly love me as a close friend?"

The change in wording gets Peter's attention. John cues us in on Peter's damaged feelings in the second half of verse 17.

> ... PETER WAS HURT BECAUSE JESUS ASKED HIM THE THIRD TIME, "DO YOU LOVE ME?"

Jesus' change from "agape" to "phileo" lands differently in Peter's shame. We can imagine tears welling up in the man's eyes as he responds to His Lord.

He said, "Lord, you know all things; you know that I love you.

Here, the Greek gives us some additional context again. The first time Peter says, "you know," he is using the Greek verb, "ginosko." It means to understand and acknowledge a fact that is known fully. Peter is saying, "Jesus, you fully and completely understand all things." Then, Peter shifts back to the "oida" verb he had previously used. He says, "You have seen through my actions."

"You have experienced it already."

Essentially, Peter makes a bold proclamation of hurt to Jesus.

> "LORD, YOU KNOW [AND COMPLETELY UNDERSTAND] ALL THINGS; YOU KNOW [AND YOU HAVE SEEN THROUGH MY PAST ACTIONS, YOU HAVE EXPERIENCED] THAT I LOVE YOU [PHILEO LOVE YOU, DEEPLY LOVE YOU LIKE A CLOSE BROTHER].

Peter humbly admits his limits as he acknowledges he could not die for Jesus as he originally said. Yet, and this is so important, Peter still loves Jesus as intimately as possible in his weakness.

Finally, in verse 18, we read a, "very truly…" statement from Jesus. These, "very truly," statements come from the Greek ἀμήν amēn.[171] At the end of a sentence, this word means, "so be it," it is used as a statement of agreement, for example, when we pray together.

However, ἀμήν amēn, used at the beginning of a sentence, as Jesus does here and elsewhere, has the power of prefacing a statement as absolute and indisputable fact.

When we read verse 18, it is important to understand Jesus is not asking for agreement; He is making a statement of fact that foretells Peter's new future.

> [18] VERY TRULY I TELL YOU, WHEN YOU WERE YOUNGER YOU DRESSED YOURSELF AND WENT WHERE YOU WANTED; BUT WHEN YOU ARE OLD YOU WILL STRETCH OUT YOUR HANDS, AND SOMEONE ELSE WILL DRESS YOU AND LEAD YOU WHERE YOU DO NOT WANT TO GO." [19] JESUS SAID THIS TO INDICATE THE KIND OF DEATH BY WHICH PETER WOULD GLORIFY GOD.

Then, in light of this foretelling of Peter's eventual martyrdom, Jesus calls Peter back to the beginning. We can imagine how these words must have landed anew on the restored Peter. Jesus looks at Peter, with complete and forgiving love. Then, Jesus restores Peter using the words He spoke to the apostle at the beginning of their relationship.

> THEN HE SAID TO HIM, "FOLLOW ME!"[172]

Jesus says to Peter, "You will be faithful to the very end, even to death... so, 'Follow me!'"

Hope

Understanding how Jesus restores Peter helps us understand the power of hope. Peter is despairing. He is examining his failings and seems lost; He goes back to his old ways. Yet, into his self-made despair, Jesus speaks and calls Him to start over and finish strong.

Jesus breathes hope back into Peter's life.

We can almost feel the restoration of hope in Peter's writing, in 1 Peter 1:22-25.

> 22 HAVING PURIFIED YOUR SOULS BY YOUR OBEDIENCE TO THE TRUTH FOR A SINCERE BROTHERLY LOVE, LOVE ONE ANOTHER EARNESTLY FROM A PURE HEART, 23 SINCE YOU HAVE BEEN BORN AGAIN, NOT OF PERISHABLE SEED BUT OF IMPERISHABLE, THROUGH THE LIVING AND ABIDING WORD OF GOD...[173]

In Jesus, Peter finds hope that allows him to love others from a pure heart. An everlasting seed of faith gets planted in his heart and bears tremendous fruit.

Peter becomes a giver of hope.

Yet, Peter's story also leaves us with a challenging faith question to ponder: If we have this complete, fully loving, always forgiving, mercy-filled love of Jesus available to us, then how does it change our lives today?

For many, it reminds us that we can always find lasting and steadfast hope in Jesus Christ. We can find hope even in despair because we have the eternal promise of forgiveness. We are reminded that our mistakes, imperfections, omissions, and sins are no more.

All our faults are gone. We are entirely free.

Hope stems from having a personal relationship with Jesus Christ.

In Him, we are completely forgiven.

We are forgiven of pride.

We are forgiven of envy.

We are forgiven of gossip.

We are forgiven of anger.

We are forgiven of addiction.

We are forgiven of murder.

We are forgiven of lust.

We are forgiven of lies.

We are forgiven of judging one another.

In all things, we are forgiven.

As the joy of forgiveness washes over us, we fully acknowledge and accept we are loved. We are not simply loved like a close friend, no. God Himself completely and sacrificially loves us.

Yes.

Despite our imperfections and faults, we have been completely and eternally forgiven.

Our sins are no more.

They are washed away.

All of our wrongs are destroyed by God's perfect light, His life, His love.

We are, finally, left with this calling to take what we know and share it. We are to pass hope to others in despair.

Like torch carriers in a cave of darkness, we become bearers of hope to a despairing world.

As we go, we become a part of God's Kingdom. We become His super-organism. We work together and take the light into the darkness. We become a fulfillment of something else Peter wrote.

This is 1 Peter 2:9-10:

> [9] BUT YOU ARE A CHOSEN PEOPLE, A ROYAL PRIESTHOOD, A HOLY NATION, GOD'S SPECIAL POSSESSION, THAT YOU MAY DECLARE THE PRAISES OF HIM WHO CALLED YOU OUT OF DARKNESS INTO HIS WONDERFUL LIGHT. [10] ONCE YOU WERE NOT A PEOPLE, BUT NOW YOU ARE THE PEOPLE OF GOD; ONCE YOU HAD NOT RECEIVED MERCY, BUT NOW YOU HAVE RECEIVED MERCY.[174]

Under His mercy, we become His unified people!

This mercy and this calling, are the very reason Jesus commanded us in the final verses of Matthew 28 to tell others about living in His radical way of agape, self-sacrificing love!

> [18] THEN JESUS CAME TO THEM AND SAID, "ALL AUTHORITY IN HEAVEN AND ON EARTH HAS BEEN GIVEN TO ME. [19] THEREFORE GO AND MAKE DISCIPLES OF ALL NATIONS, BAPTIZING THEM IN THE NAME OF THE FATHER AND OF THE SON AND OF THE HOLY SPIRIT, [20] AND TEACHING THEM TO OBEY EVERYTHING I HAVE COMMANDED YOU. AND SURELY I AM WITH YOU ALWAYS, TO THE VERY END OF THE AGE."[175]

Do you hear the hope in His Great Commision?

He has given us purpose.

He has given us hope.

He is, as He says, with us, "always!"

Where, then, will you place your hope?

Who will you tell?

Who do you love enough to share true and eternal hope?

FOOTNOTES

1. ˆ Piper, J. (2023, August 18). *What is hope?*. Desiring God. https://www.desiringgod.org/messages/what-is-hope.
2. ˆ Bumpus, J. D. (2021, June 25). *Elvis Presley: Why the king joked about his necklace he wore in the final years of his life*. Outsider. https://outsider.com/entertainment/elvis-presley-why-king-joked-necklace-he-wore-final-years-life/
3. ˆ Ibid.
4. ˆ *The New International Version*. (2011). (Is 42:1–7). Grand Rapids, MI: Zondervan.
5. ˆ VanGemeren, Willem A. "Isaiah," in *Evangelical Commentary on the Bible*, vol. 3, Baker Reference Library (Grand Rapids, MI: Baker Book House, 1995), 471.
6. ˆ Ibid. (Is 42:1).
7. ˆ Ibid. (Mt 12:21).
8. ˆ Ibid. (Mt 1:1–25).
9. ˆ Gap, J. (2013, September 6). *The secret to the modern beehive is a one-centimeter air gap*. Smithsonian.com. https://www.smithsonianmag.com/arts-culture/the-secret-to-the-modern-beehive-is-a-one-centimeter-air-gap-4427011.
10. ˆ The entrance reducer is a tool to prevent other bees, and pests, from attacking or robbing honeybees.
11. ˆ *The Holy Bible: English Standard Version* (Wheaton, IL: Crossway Bibles, 2016), Ge 1:1–3.
12. ˆ Eugene H. Peterson,*The Message: The Bible in Contemporary Language* (Colorado Springs, CO: NavPress, 2005), Ps 19:1–9.
13. ˆ *The Holy Bible: English Standard Version* (Wheaton, IL: Crossway Bibles, 2016), Heb 11:1–3.
14. ˆ Ibid. Jn 1:1–5.
15. ˆ "Ars Honey Bee Health." index: USDA ARS. Accessed August 15, 2023. https://www.ars.usda.gov/oc/br/ccd/index/.
16. ˆ Borenstein, S. (2023, June 27). *Nearly half of US honeybee colonies died last year. struggling beekeepers stabilize population*. AP News. https://apnews.com/article/honeybees-pollinator-extinct-disease-death-climate-change-f60297706e19c7346ff1881587b5aced

17. ^ Ibid.
18. ^ Ibid.
19. ^ López-Incera, A., Nouvian, M., Ried, K. *et al.* Honeybee communication during collective defence is shaped by predation. *BMC Biol* 19, 106 (2021). https://doi.org/10.1186/s12915-021-01028-x
20. ^ McGivney, Annette. *"Bees Are Sentient': Inside the Stunning Brains of Nature's Hardest Workers."* The Guardian, April 2, 2023. https://www.theguardian.com/environment/2023/apr/02/bees-intelligence-minds-pollination.
21. ^ Ibid.
22. ^ Ibid.
23. ^ Ibid.
24. ^ *Oxford languages and google - english*. Oxford Languages. (n.d.). https://languages.oup.com/google-dictionary-en/
25. ^ *Despair*. DESPAIR | definition in the Cambridge English Dictionary. (n.d.). https://dictionary.cambridge.org/us/dictionary/english/despair
26. ^ *The Holy Bible: English Standard Version* (Wheaton, IL: Crossway Bibles, 2016), Ge 3:1–7.
27. ^ Tzu, Sun. 2010. *The Art of War*. PDF. Capstone Classics. Chichester, England: Capstone Publishing.
28. ^ *The Holy Bible: English Standard Version* (Wheaton, IL: Crossway Bibles, 2016), 1 Pe 5:8.
29. ^ Wiersbe, Warren. 1979. *The Strategy of Satan: How to Detect and Defeat Him*. Tyndale House Publishers.
30. ^ Anton, K., & Krozinger, C. (n.d.). *An introduction to queen honey bee development*. Penn State Extension. https://extension.psu.edu/an-introduction-to-queen-honey-bee-development
31. ^ Ibid.
32. ^ *Stages of bee growth*. Honey Bee Research Centre. (n.d.). https://hbrc.ca/stages-of-bee-growth/
33. ^ Ibid.
34. ^ Mortensen, A. N., Ellis, J. D., & Smith, B. (n.d.). *The Social Organization of Bees*. Eny-166/IN1102: The Social Organization of Honey Bees. https://edis.ifas.ufl.edu/publication/IN1102
35. ^ Ibid.
36. ^ Rutter, B. (2023, May 19). *3 levels of bee hierarchy: Drone Bee, worker Bee, and Queen Bee*. The Best Bees Company. https://bestbees.com/2022/05/19/bee-hierarchy/
37. ^ Forbes Magazine. (2012, July 11). *Full list: America's most expensive ZIP codes*. Forbes. https://www.forbes.com/2009/08/26/most-expensive-zip-codes-lifestyle-real-estate-zip_full-list.html

38. ˄ Mathisen, Ralph W. *Peregrini, Barbari*, and *Cives Romani*: Concepts of Citizenship and the Legal Identity of Barbarians in the Later Roman Empire, *The American Historical Review*, Volume 111, Issue 4, October 2006, Pages 1011–1040, https://doi.org/10.1086/ahr.111.4.1011
39. ˄ *The New International Version* (Grand Rapids, MI: Zondervan, 2011), Lk 6:17–26.
40. ˄ Ibid. Lk 6:17–26.
41. ˄ Expositor's Bible Commentary: Matthew, Mark, Luke. pg. 891
42. ˄ Ibid. pg. 891
43. ˄ Aberbach, David (2018). *Poverty and mass education: The Jews in the Roman empire, Working Paper Series, No. 18-192*, London School of Economics and Political Science (LSE), Department of International Development, London
44. ˄ Redding, Jonathan D. "Wealth," ed. Douglas Mangum et al., *Lexham Theological Wordbook*, Lexham Bible Reference Series (Bellingham, WA: Lexham Press, 2014).
45. ˄ Strong, James.*A Concise Dictionary of the Words in the Greek Testament and The Hebrew Bible* (Bellingham, WA: Logos Bible Software, 2009), 58.
46. ˄ Expositor's Bible Commentary: Matthew, Mark, Luke. pg. 892
47. ˄ Ibid.
48. ˄ Ibid. Lk 6:17–26.
49. ˄ *The New International Version* (Grand Rapids, MI: Zondervan, 2011), Lk 6:17–26.
50. ˄ Ibid. Lk 6:17–26.
51. ˄ Ibid. (Mt 5:6).
52. ˄ Marchetti, S. (2020, November 25). *Lying down and vomiting between courses: This is how ancient romans would feast*. CNN. https://www.cnn.com/style/article/ancient-roman-feasting-history/index.html
53. ˄ Ibid.
54. ˄ Always check with a medical professional before fasting from food or other sustenance.
55. ˄ *The New International Version* (Grand Rapids, MI: Zondervan, 2011), Lk 6:17–26.
56. ˄ Ibid. (Lk 6:17–26).
57. ˄ Expositor's Bible Commentary: Matthew, Mark, Luke. pg. 891
58. ˄ *The New International Version*. (2011). (Lk 18:1–8). Grand Rapids, MI: Zondervan.
59. ˄ Harvey, A. (2023, May 3). *How do bees make honey? from the hive to the pot*. LiveScience. https://www.livescience.com/how-do-bees-make-honey
60. ˄ *Honey Bee Swarms*. TN Department of Agriculture. (n.d.). https://www.tn.gov/agriculture/businesses/bees/honey-bee-swarms.
61. ˄ Ibid.

FOOTNOTES

62. ^ Harvey, A. (2023, May 3). *How do bees make honey? from the hive to the pot.* LiveScience. https://www.livescience.com/how-do-bees-make-honey
63. ^ Berthold, E. (2018, August 4). What it takes to make a queen bee. https://www.science.org.au/curious/earth-environment/what-it-takes-make-queen-bee
64. ^ Bakour, Meryem et al. "Bee Bread as a Promising Source of Bioactive Molecules and Functional Properties: An Up-To-Date Review." *Antibiotics (Basel, Switzerland)* vol. 11,2 203. 5 Feb. 2022, doi:10.3390/antibiotics11020203
65. ^ Wenfu Mao et al. A dietary phytochemical alters caste-associated gene expression in honey bees.*Sci. Adv.*1,e1500795(2015).DOI:10.1126/sciadv.1500795
66. ^ Harvey, A. (2023, May 3). *How do bees make honey? from the hive to the pot.* LiveScience. https://www.livescience.com/how-do-bees-make-honey
67. ^ Ibid.
68. ^ Ibid.
69. ^ Ibid.
70. ^ Heidinger IM, Meixner MD, Berg S, Büchler R. Observation of the Mating Behavior of Honey Bee (Apis mellifera L.) Queens Using Radio-Frequency Identification (RFID): Factors Influencing the Duration and Frequency of Nuptial Flights. Insects. 2014 Jul 1;5(3):513-27. doi: 10.3390/insects5030513. PMID: 26462822; PMCID: PMC4592583.
71. ^ Ibid.
72. ^ *The New International Version.* (2011). (Ro 12:1–2). Grand Rapids, MI: Zondervan.
73. ^ Tolkien, J. R. R. 1991. *The Fellowship of the Ring.* The Lord of the Rings 1. London, England: HarperCollins.
74. ^ *The New International Version.* (2011). (2 Co 4:5–6). Grand Rapids, MI: Zondervan.
75. ^ Ibid. (Lk 24:50–53).
76. ^ Ibid. (Lk 1:1–4).
77. ^ Ibid. (Ac 1:1–2).
78. ^ John A. Martin, "Luke," in *The Bible Knowledge Commentary: An Exposition of the Scriptures*, ed. J. F. Walvoord and R. B. Zuck, vol. 2 (Wheaton, IL: Victor Books, 1985), 202.
79. ^ Ibid. (Ac 1:3-5).
80. ^ Ibid. (Ac 1:6-8).
81. ^ Ibid. (Ac 1:8).
82. ^ Ibid. (Ac 1:8).
83. ^ Snow, A. (2023, August 6). *Why jerusalem, judea, and samaria?.* FIRM Israel. https://firmisrael.org/learn/why-jerusalem-judea-and-samaria/
84. ^ *The New International Version.* (2011). (Ac 1:1). Grand Rapids, MI: Zondervan.

85. ˆ Ibid. (Ac 1:9-11).
86. ˆ Wagh, Vijay D. "Propolis: a wonder bees product and its pharmacological potentials." *Advances in pharmacological sciences* vol. 2013 (2013): 308249. doi:10.1155/2013/308249
87. ˆ Wenseleers, Tom. (2009). The Superorganism Revisited. BioScience. 59. 702-705. 10.1525/bio.2009.59.8.12.
88. ˆ Ibid.
89. ˆ Vince, G. (2022, February 24). *Homni: The new superorganism taking over Earth*. BBC Future. https://www.bbc.com/future/article/20140701-the-superorganism-engulfing-earth
90. ˆ Ibid.
91. ˆ *The colony and its organization*. Mid-Atlantic Apiculture Research and Extension Consortium. (n.d.). https://canr.udel.edu/maarec/honey-bee-biology/the-colony-and-its-organization.
92. ˆ Ibid.
93. ˆ Ibid.
94. ˆ *About honey bees: Types, races, and Anatomy of Honey Bees*. About Honey Bees | Types, races, and anatomy of honey bees. (n.d.). https://www.uaex.uada.edu/farm-ranch/special-programs/beekeeping/about-honey-bees.aspx
95. ˆ Ibid.
96. ˆ Currie RW. The biology and behaviour of drones. *Bee World*. 1987;68:129 –143.
97. ˆ Ibid.
98. ˆ *Drone honey bee: The ecstasy and the agony*. Wisconsin Pollinators. (n.d.). https://wisconsinpollinators.com/Bee/BA_HoneyBeeDrone.aspx
99. ˆ Ibid.
100. ˆ Ibid.
101. ˆ Ibid.
102. ˆ *About honey bees: Types, races, and Anatomy of Honey Bees*. About Honey Bees | Types, races, and anatomy of honey bees. (n.d.). https://www.uaex.uada.edu/farm-ranch/special-programs/beekeeping/about-honey-bees.aspx
103. ˆ *The colony and its organization*. Mid-Atlantic Apiculture Research and Extension Consortium. (n.d.). https://canr.udel.edu/maarec/honey-bee-biology/the-colony-and-its-organization/#:~:text=A%20honey%20bee%20colony%20typically,%2C%20drones%2C%20and%20a%20queen.
104. ˆ López-Uribe, M. (n.d.-a). *Where do bee pollinators go during the winter?*. Penn State Extension. https://extension.psu.edu/where-do-bee-pollinators-go-during-the-winter
105. ˆ Ibid.

FOOTNOTES

106. ^ *About honey bees: Types, races, and Anatomy of Honey Bees*. About Honey Bees | Types, races, and anatomy of honey bees. (n.d.). https://www.uaex.uada.edu/farm-ranch/special-programs/beekeeping/about-honey-bees.aspx
107. ^ Anton, K., & Grozinger, C. (n.d.). *An introduction to queen honey bee development*. Penn State Extension. https://extension.psu.edu/an-introduction-to-queen-honey-bee-development#:~:text=Healthy%2C%20fertile%20queens%20are%20capable,the%20first%20year%20or%20two.
108. ^ Ibid.
109. ^ Ibid.
110. ^ "The constitution [of the United Arab Emirates (U.A.E.)] designates Islam as the official religion. It guarantees freedom of worship as long as it does not conflict with public policy or morals. It states all persons are equal before the law, and prohibits discrimination on grounds of religious belief. The law prohibits blasphemy, proselytizing by non-Muslims, and conversion from Islam."

    Source: U.S. Department of State. (2020, December 1). *United Arab Emirates - United States Department of State*. U.S. Department of State. https://www.state.gov/reports/2018-report-on-international-religious-freedom/united-arab-emirates/#:~:text=It%20states%20all%20persons%20are,Muslims%2C%20and%20conversion%20from%20Islam.
111. ^ *The New International Version*. (2011). (1 Co 1:10–17). Grand Rapids, MI: Zondervan.
112. ^ Spicq, C., & Ernest, J. D. (1994).*Theological lexicon of the New Testament* (Vol. 3, p. 321). Peabody, MA: Hendrickson Publishers.
113. ^ Ceslas Spicq and James D. Ernest,*Theological Lexicon of the New Testament* (Peabody, MA: Hendrickson Publishers, 1994), 321.
114. ^ *The New International Version*. (2011). (Ro 6:5–7). Grand Rapids, MI: Zondervan.
115. ^ Luke 6:13-16: [13] When morning came, he called his disciples to him and chose twelve of them, whom he also designated apostles: [14] Simon (whom he named Peter), his brother Andrew, James, John, Philip, Bartholomew, [15] Matthew, Thomas, James son of Alphaeus, Simon who was called the Zealot, [16] Judas son of James, and Judas Iscariot, who became a traitor. - *The New International Version*. (2011). (Lk 6:13–16). Grand Rapids, MI: Zondervan.
116. ^ *The New International Version*. (2011). (Eph 4:1–6). Grand Rapids, MI: Zondervan.
117. ^ *How honey is made*. National Honey Board. (n.d.). https://honey.com/about-honey/how-honey-is-made#:~:text=Honey%20starts%20as%20flower%20nectar,nectar%20collected%20by%20the%20bees.

118. ^ Nicolson, S. W., Human, H., & Pirk, C. W. (2022). Honey bees save energy in honey processing by dehydrating nectar before returning to the nest. *Scientific Reports, 12*(1), 1-8. https://doi.org/10.1038/s41598-022-20626-5
119. ^ De Marco RJ, Farina WM. *Trophallaxis in forager honeybees (Apis mellifera): resource uncertainty enhances begging contacts?* J Comp Physiol A Neuroethol Sens Neural Behav Physiol. 2003 Feb;189(2):125-34. doi: 10.1007/s00359-002-0382-y. Epub 2003 Jan 24. PMID: 12607041.
120. ^ Nicolson, S. W., Human, H., & Pirk, C. W. (2022). Honey bees save energy in honey processing by dehydrating nectar before returning to the nest. *Scientific Reports, 12*(1), 1-8. https://doi.org/10.1038/s41598-022-20626-5
121. ^ *How honey is made.* National Honey Board. (n.d.). https://honey.com/about-honey/how-honey-is-made#:~:text=Honey%20starts%20as%20flower%20nectar,nectar%20collected%20by%20the%20bees.
122. ^ Ibid.
123. ^ Nicolson, S. W., Human, H., & Pirk, C. W. (2022). Honey bees save energy in honey processing by dehydrating nectar before returning to the nest. *Scientific Reports, 12*(1), 1-8. https://doi.org/10.1038/s41598-022-20626-5
124. ^ *How honey is made.* National Honey Board. (n.d.). https://honey.com/about-honey/how-honey-is-made#:~:text=Honey%20starts%20as%20flower%20nectar,nectar%20collected%20by%20the%20bees.
125. ^ Ibid.
126. ^ Ibid.
127. ^ Ibid.
128. ^ Ibid.
129. ^ Ibid.
130. ^ Evans, D. (2022, October 11). *Beekeeping Economics.* The Apiarist. https://theapiarist.org/beekeeping-economics/
131. ^ Jernigan, Christopher M. (2017, June 13). Honey and the Hive. ASU - Ask A Biologist. Retrieved August 25, 2023 from https://askabiologist.asu.edu/bee-honey
132. ^ Jernigan, Christopher M. (2017, June 13). Honey and the Hive. ASU - Ask A Biologist. Retrieved August 25, 2023 from https://askabiologist.asu.edu/bee-honey
133. ^ *How to make a pound of Honey.* Canadian Honey Council. (n.d.). https://honeycouncil.ca/how-to-make-a-pound-of-honey/
134. ^ Ibid.
135. ^ Ibid.
136. ^ *Bee Curious.* Sioux Honey Association Co-Op. (2020, August 26). https://siouxhoney.com/bee-curious

FOOTNOTES

137. ˄ *Bee Curious*. Sioux Honey Association Co-Op. (2020, August 26). https://siouxhoney.com/bee-curious
138. ˄ Taft, M. (n.d.). *Bee is for biodiversity*. Defenders of Wildlife. https://defenders.org/blog/2021/05/bee-biodiversity
139. ˄ *The Holy Bible: English Standard Version*. (2016). (Mt 9:35–38). Wheaton, IL: Crossway Bibles.
140. ˄ Ibid. (Ge 2:7–9).
141. ˄ *The New International Version* (Grand Rapids, MI: Zondervan, 2011), Ge 1:31.
142. ˄ *The Holy Bible: English Standard Version*. (2016). (Re 14:14–16). Wheaton, IL: Crossway Bibles.
143. ˄ Ibid. (Mt 9:35–38).
144. ˄ Ibid. (Lk 9:57–10:3).
145. ˄ Barbieri, L. A., Jr. (1985). Matthew. In J. F. Walvoord & R. B. Zuck (Eds.), *The Bible Knowledge Commentary: An Exposition of the Scriptures* (Vol. 2, p. 41). Wheaton, IL: Victor Books.
146. ˄ *The Holy Bible: English Standard Version*. (2016). (Mt 9:35). Wheaton, IL: Crossway Bibles.
147. ˄ Ibid. (Mt 9:36).
148. ˄ Ibid.
149. ˄ Ibid. (Mt. 9:37-38)
150. ˄ Ibid. (Jn 4:31–38).
151. ˄ France, R. T. (1994). Matthew. In D. A. Carson, R. T. France, J. A. Motyer, & G. J. Wenham (Eds.), *New Bible commentary: 21st century edition* (4th ed., pp. 916–917). Leicester, England; Downers Grove, IL: Inter-Varsity Press.
152. ˄ *The Holy Bible: English Standard Version*. (2016). (Mt 9:35–38). Wheaton, IL: Crossway Bibles.
153. ˄ *The New International Version* (Grand Rapids, MI: Zondervan, 2011), Jn 21:5–6.
154. ˄ Ibid. *(*Jn 21:7).
155. ˄ Ibid. (Jn 1:40–42).
156. ˄ Ibid. (Jn 1:43).
157. ˄ Ibid. (Mt 16:13–20).
158. ˄ Ibid. (Jn 13:33).
159. ˄ Ibid. (Jn 13:34–38).
160. ˄ Ibid. (Jn 13:36-37).
161. ˄ Ibid. (Jn 13:38).
162. ˄ Ibid. (Mt 16:13–20).
163. ˄ Ibid. (Jn 21:15).
164. ˄ ἀγαπάω (*agapaō*). vb. to love. *Involves a deep level of affection and intimacy.*

This verb is the usual Septuagint translation of Hebrew אָהַב (*'āhab*, "to love"). It occurs frequently in the nt, much more often than φιλέω (*phileō*, "to love"). The verb *agapaō* can describe Jesus' love for people (e.g., Mark 10:21), the Father's love for Jesus (e.g., John 3:35), human love for God (e.g., Mark 12:30) and a broader range of love between people, including love for one's neighbor and even one's enemy (e.g., Matt 5:43–46).

Source: Justin Langford,"Friendship," ed. Douglas Mangum et al., *Lexham Theological Wordbook*, Lexham Bible Reference Series (Bellingham, WA: Lexham Press, 2014).

165. ^ *The New International Version* (Grand Rapids, MI: Zondervan, 2011), (Jn 12:43).
166. ^ Ibid. (Jn 13:34-35).
167. ^ Ibid. (Jn 21:15b).
168. ^ οἶδα (*oida*). vb. to have seen, to know. *Refers to the past act of seeing with the present effect of knowing what was seen.*

Technically a perfect tense from εἶδον (*eidon*, "see") but used as a present (see bdag, s.v. οἶδα), *oida* occurs over 300 times in the nt. To "have seen" something in the past becomes "to know" it in the present. *Oida* often connotes not only having knowledge but also being able to understand that knowledge (Luke 2:49; Acts 3:17; Rom 6:9).

Source: Jeremiah K. Garrett,"Knowledge," ed. Douglas Mangum et al., *Lexham Theological Wordbook*, Lexham Bible Reference Series (Bellingham, WA: Lexham Press, 2014).

169. ^ φιλέω (*phileō*). vb. to love, like, or kiss. *Describes an affection ranging from general emotion to deep love.*

While the term can convey deep affection for another person, the range of meaning is probably narrower than αγαπάω (*agapaō*, "to love"). The type of love expressed by *phileō* can be found among relatives (Matt 10:37) and friends (John 11:3); *phileō* can also describe God's love for Christ (John 5:20).

Source: Justin Langford,"Friendship," ed. Douglas Mangum et al., *Lexham Theological Wordbook*, Lexham Bible Reference Series (Bellingham, WA: Lexham Press, 2014).

170. ^ ἀρνίον (originally, *a little lamb*, but diminutive force was lost), *a lamb*: see ἀρήν. Souter, A. (1917).*A Pocket Lexicon to the Greek New Testament* (p. 37). Oxford: Clarendon Press.
171. ^ ἀμήν amēn, *am-ane'*; of Heb. or. [543]; prop. *firm*, i.e. (fig.) *trustworthy*; adv. *surely* (often as interj. *so be it*):—amen, verily.

Source: James Strong,*A Concise Dictionary of the Words in the Greek Testament and The Hebrew Bible* (Bellingham, WA: Logos Bible Software, 2009), 10.
172. ^ *The New International Version*. (2011). (Jn 21:15–25). Grand Rapids, MI: Zondervan.

FOOTNOTES

173. ^ *The Holy Bible: English Standard Version*. (2016). (1 Pe 1:22–25). Wheaton, IL: Crossway Bibles.
174. ^ *The New International Version*. (2011). (1 Pe 2:9–10). Grand Rapids, MI: Zondervan.
175. ^ Ibid. (Mt 28:18–20).

SOURCES

Aberbach, David (2018): *Poverty and mass education: The Jews in the Roman empire, Working Paper Series, No. 18-192*, London School of Economics and Political Science (LSE), Department of International Development, London

About honey bees: Types, races, and Anatomy of Honey Bees. About Honey Bees | Types, races, and anatomy of honey bees. (n.d.). https://www.uaex.uada.edu/farm-ranch/special-programs/beekeeping/about-honey-bees.aspx.

Anton, K., & Krozinger, C. (n.d.). *An introduction to queen honey bee development*. Penn State Extension. https://extension.psu.edu/an-introduction-to-queen-honey-bee-development.

"Ars Honey Bee Health." index: USDA ARS. Accessed August 15, 2023. https://www.ars.usda.gov/oc/br/ccd/index.

Bakour, Meryem et al. "Bee Bread as a Promising Source of Bioactive Molecules and Functional Properties: An Up-To-Date Review." *Antibiotics (Basel, Switzerland)* vol. 11,2 203. 5 Feb. 2022, doi:10.3390/antibiotics11020203

Barbieri, L. A., Jr. (1985). Matthew. In J. F. Walvoord & R. B. Zuck (Eds.), *The Bible Knowledge Commentary: An Exposition of the Scriptures* (Vol. 2, p. 41). Wheaton, IL: Victor Books.

Bee Curious. Sioux Honey Association Co-Op. (2020, August 26). https://siouxhoney.com/bee-curious.

Berthold, E. (2018, August 4). What it takes to make a queen bee. https://www.science.org.au/curious/earth-environment/what-it-takes-make-queen-bee.

SOURCES

Borenstein, S. (2023, June 27). *Nearly half of US honeybee colonies died last year. struggling beekeepers stabilize population*. AP News.https://apnews.com/article/honeybees-pollinator-extinct-disease-death-climate-change-f60297706e19c7346ff1881587b5aced.

Bumpus, J. D. (2021, June 25). *Elvis Presley: Why the king joked about his necklace he wore in the final years of his life*. Outsider. https://outsider.com/entertainment/elvis-presley-why-king-joked-necklace-he-wore-final-years-life.

Cambridge English Dictionary. DESPAIR | definition in the Cambridge English Dictionary. (n.d.). https://dictionary.cambridge.org/us/dictionary/english/despair.

Ceslas Spicq and James D. Ernest, *Theological Lexicon of the New Testament* (Peabody, MA: Hendrickson Publishers, 1994), 321.

Currie RW. The biology and behaviour of drones. *Bee World*. 1987;68:129–143.

Eugene H. Peterson, *The Message: The Bible in Contemporary Language* (Colorado Springs, CO: NavPress, 2005), Ps 19:1–9.

Evans, D. (2022, October 11). *Beekeeping Economics*. The Apiarist. https://theapiarist.org/beekeeping-economics.

Expositor's Bible Commentary: Matthew, Mark, Luke. pg. 891.

De Marco RJ, Farina WM. *Trophallaxis in forager honeybees (Apis mellifera): resource uncertainty enhances begging contacts?* J Comp Physiol A Neuroethol Sens Neural Behav Physiol. 2003 Feb;189(2):125-34. doi: 10.1007/s00359-002-0382-y. Epub 2003 Jan 24. PMID: 12607041.

Drone honey bee: The ecstasy and the agony. Wisconsin Pollinators. (n.d.). https://wisconsinpollinators.com/Bee/BA_HoneyBeeDrone.aspx

Forbes Magazine. (2012, July 11). *Full list: America's most expensive ZIP codes*. Forbes. https://www.forbes.com/2009/08/26/most-expensive-zip-codes-lifestyle-real-estate-zip_full-list.html

France, R. T. (1994). Matthew. In D. A. Carson, R. T. France, J. A. Motyer, & G. J. Wenham (Eds.), *New Bible commentary: 21st century edition* (4th ed., pp. 916–917). Leicester, England; Downers Grove, IL: Inter-Varsity Press.

Free, J. B., & Williams, I. H. (1975). Factors determining the rearing and rejection of drones by the honeybee colony. *Animal Behaviour, 23*, 650-675.

Gap, J. (2013, September 6). *The secret to the modern beehive is a one-centimeter air gap*. Smithsonian.com. https://www.smithsonianmag.com/arts-culture/the-secret-to-the-modern-beehive-is-a-one-centimeter-air-gap-4427011.

Garrett, Jeremiah K. "Knowledge," ed. Douglas Mangum et al., *Lexham Theological Wordbook*, Lexham Bible Reference Series (Bellingham, WA: Lexham Press, 2014).

Harvey, A. (2023, May 3). *How do bees make honey? from the hive to the pot*. LiveScience. https://www.livescience.com/how-do-bees-make-honey.

Heidinger IM, Meixner MD, Berg S, Büchler R. Observation of the Mating Behavior of Honey Bee (Apis mellifera L.) Queens Using Radio-Frequency Identification (RFID): Factors Influencing the Duration and Frequency of Nuptial Flights. Insects. 2014 Jul 1;5(3):513-27. doi: 10.3390/insects5030513. PMID: 26462822; PMCID: PMC4592583.

Honey Bee Swarms. TN Department of Agriculture. (n.d.). https://www.tn.gov/agriculture/businesses/bees/honey-bee-swarms.html.

How honey is made. National Honey Board. (n.d.). https://honey.com/about-honey/how-honey-is-made.

How to make a pound of Honey. Canadian Honey Council. (n.d.). https://honeycouncil.ca/how-to-make-a-pound-of-honey.

Jernigan, Christopher M. (2017, June 13). Honey and the Hive. ASU - Ask A Biologist. Retrieved August 25, 2023 from https://askabiologist.asu.edu/bee-honey.

SOURCES

Langford, Justin. "Friendship," ed. Douglas Mangum et al., *Lexham Theological Wordbook*, Lexham Bible Reference Series (Bellingham, WA: Lexham Press, 2014).

López-Incera, A., Nouvian, M., Ried, K. *et al.* Honeybee communication during collective defence is shaped by predation. *BMC Biol* 19, 106 (2021). https://doi.org/10.1186/s12915-021-01028-x

López-Uribe, M. (n.d.-a). *Where do bee pollinators go during the winter?*. Penn State Extension. https://extension.psu.edu/where-do-bee-pollinators-go-during-the-winter.

Mathisen, Ralph W. *Peregrini, Barbari,* and *Cives Romani*: Concepts of Citizenship and the Legal Identity of Barbarians in the Later Roman Empire, *The American Historical Review*, Volume 111, Issue 4, October 2006, Pages 1011–1040, https://doi.org/10.1086/ahr.111.4.1011

Marchetti, S. (2020, November 25). *Lying down and vomiting between courses: This is how ancient romans would feast*. CNN. https://www.cnn.com/style/article/ancient-roman-feasting-history/index.html.

Martin, John A. "Luke," in *The Bible Knowledge Commentary: An Exposition of the Scriptures*, ed. J. F. Walvoord and R. B. Zuck, vol. 2 (Wheaton, IL: Victor Books, 1985), 202.

McGivney, Annette. *"'Bees Are Sentient': Inside the Stunning Brains of Nature's Hardest Workers."* The Guardian, April 2, 2023. https://www.theguardian.com/environment/2023/apr/02/bees-intelligence-minds-pollination.

Mortensen, A. N., Ellis, J. D., & Smith, B. (n.d.). *The Social Organization of Bees*. Eny-166/IN1102: The Social Organization of Honey Bees. https://edis.ifas.ufl.edu/publication/IN1102.

Nicolson, S. W., Human, H., & Pirk, C. W. (2022). *Honey bees save energy in honey processing by dehydrating nectar before returning to the nest*. Scientific Reports, 12(1), 1-8. https://doi.org/10.1038/s41598-022-20626-5.

Oxford languages and google - english. Oxford Languages. (n.d.). https://languages.oup.com/google-dictionary-en.

SOURCES

Rutter, B. (2023, May 19). *3 levels of bee hierarchy: Drone Bee, worker Bee, and Queen Bee*. The Best Bees Company. https://bestbees.com/2022/05/19/bee-hierarchy.

Souter, A. (1917).*A Pocket Lexicon to the Greek New Testament* (p. 37). Oxford: Clarendon Press.

Spicq, C., & Ernest, J. D. (1994).*Theological lexicon of the New Testament* (Vol. 3, p. 321). Peabody, MA: Hendrickson Publishers.
Stages of bee growth. Honey Bee Research Centre. (n.d.). https://hbrc.ca/stages-of-bee-growth.

The colony and its organization. Mid-Atlantic Apiculture Research and Extension Consortium. (n.d.). https://canr.udel.edu/maarec/honey-bee-biology/the-colony-and-its-organization.

The Holy Bible: English Standard Version. (2016). Wheaton, IL: Crossway Bibles.

The New International Version. (2011). Grand Rapids, MI: Zondervan.

Tzu, Sun. 2010. *The Art of War*. PDF. Capstone Classics. Chichester, England: Capstone Publishing.

U.S. Department of State. (2020, December 1). *United Arab Emirates - United States Department of State*. U.S. Department of State. https://www.state.gov/reports/2018-report-on-international-religious-freedom/united-arab-emirates.

Piper, J. (2023, August 18). *What is hope?*. Desiring God. https://www.desiringgod.org/messages/what-is-hope.

Redding, Jonathan D. "Wealth," ed. Douglas Mangum et al., *Lexham Theological Wordbook*, Lexham Bible Reference Series (Bellingham, WA: Lexham Press, 2014).

Rueppell, Olav et al. "Biodemographic analysis of male honey bee mortality." *Aging cell* vol. 4,1 (2005): 13-9. doi:10.1111/j.1474-9728.2004.00141.x.

SOURCES

Snow, A. (2023, August 6). *Why jerusalem, judea, and samaria?*. FIRM Israel. https://firmisrael.org/learn/why-jerusalem-judea-and-samaria.

Stankus, Tony. (2014) Reviews of Science for Science Librarians: An Update on Honeybee Colony Collapse Disorder, Science & Technology Libraries, 33:3, 228-260, DOI: 10.1080/0194262X.2014.912573.

Strong, James,*A Concise Dictionary of the Words in the Greek Testament and The Hebrew Bible* (Bellingham, WA: Logos Bible Software, 2009), 10 & 58.

Taft, M. (n.d.). *Bee is for biodiversity*. Defenders of Wildlife. https://defenders.org/blog/2021/05/bee-biodiversity.

Tolkien, J. R. R. 1991. *The Fellowship of the Ring*. The Lord of the Rings 1. London, England: HarperCollins.

Tucker, K. W. (1978). *Honey bee pests, predators, and diseases* (Vol. 410, p. 411). Cornell University Press, Ithaca, NY.

VanGemeren, Willem A. "Isaiah," in *Evangelical Commentary on the Bible*, vol. 3, Baker Reference Library (Grand Rapids, MI: Baker Book House, 1995), 471.

Vince, G. (2022, February 24). *Homni: The new superorganism taking over Earth*. BBC Future. https://www.bbc.com/future/article/20140701-the-superorganism-engulfing-earth.

Wagh, Vijay D. "Propolis: a wonder bees product and its pharmacological potentials." *Advances in pharmacological sciences* vol. 2013 (2013): 308249. doi:10.1155/2013/308249.

Walter A. Elwell, "Revelation," in *Evangelical Commentary on the Bible*, vol. 3, Baker Reference Library (Grand Rapids, MI: Baker Book House, 1995), 1213–1214.

Wenfu Mao et al. A dietary phytochemical alters caste-associated gene expression in honey bees.*Sci. Adv.*1,e1500795(2015).DOI:10.1126/sciadv.1500795.

Wenseleers, Tom. (2009). The Superorganism Revisited. BioScience. 59. 702-705. 10.1525/bio.2009.59.8.12.

Wiersbe, Warren. 1979. *The Strategy of Satan: How to Detect and Defeat Him.* Tyndale House Publishers.

Michael J. Chanley is a pastor, author, and beekeeper. He is a husband, father, and veteran of the United States Marine Corps. Alongside his family, Michael manages a small hobby farm. You can discover updates from the farm and bee-yard by following Rosecroft Farmstead on Facebook or Instagram.

As a lover of God and people, Michael has pursued an education studying both. He has earned degrees in history and sociology from Indiana University. Then, his Master's degree, from Lincoln Christian Seminary, challenged him to study ministry, spiritual formation, and leadership.

His informative and spiritually-grounded approach to writing has led to many accolades and positive reviews. His books are frequently included on "Top Seller" and "Hot New Release" lists.

Like any true extrovert, Michael accepts friend requests from people he's never met before.

You can call or text Michael at 650.636.7780.

Learn more, and find links to social media by visiting michaeljchanley.com

For speaking engagements, email emersen@churchlit.com.

www.ingramcontent.com/pod-product-compliance
Lightning Source LLC
Chambersburg PA
CBHW020656060526
44119CB00090B/409/J